Written by a young and controversial salesman Andrei Mungiu

With support from his beautiful wife Valeria Mungiu

Introduction

Congratulations on deciding to set yourself apart from the crowd by becoming a professional. Congratulations on deciding to purchase this book and aiming to become an expert in sales.

It is very important for you to learn the skills taught by this book you and how you can benefit from them. For that, read the entire introduction section to double the knowledge you get from this book.

For a start, I will give you a very brief description of my experiences that contributed to the knowledge expressed in this book.

Throughout the years, since 7 years old, observations recorded in the memory how salesmen deal with customers, behind the counter of the small company owned by the parents. Countless times, having heard how they made conclusions about weather an employee was selling well or if they should fire them, a world in which few righters have real time access to. In the process, it became more and more clear how a salesman influences people who buy & how that same salesman makes them return to the shop. One could understand why some customers never came back making huge complains and why others were happy bringing in more prospects as members of their families.

The groundbreaking observations continue to this day. Having a great time helping people from countries around the world buy solutions for their problems, I am proud of being a sales expert and it is time you become proud of your profession as well.

As time went by, my interest in how people reacted and why they reacted that way lead me to small readings on books about Body Language, Human Psychology, Neuro Linguistic Programming and other influential subjects on selling. The studies continued at the university where horizons broadened regarding many processes involved in the day-to-day business. These were subjects as Organizational Behavior, Business Strategy, Communication and other relevant courses, which became the building blocks of a future as an expert salesman & entrepreneur.

Yes, University did provide a winning edge, but it only gave the edge. I had to create the whole sword throughout my life and continuously optimize it to this point. What University has never been able to prepare for is what happened next, after graduation.

During the last two years of studies, the 2008 economic downturn dramatically affected the family business and motivation surfaced more than ever to work day & night on selling people to invest in our company. At night, we used to sit at a small desk trying to see where we could cut costs and improve the morale of workers by selling them on new ideas, by creating a fresh wave of motivation.

Even though these workers were receiving small wages, using communication skills, we managed to increase their productivity whilst still working on finding a way to expand the business. These several years dramatically changed our idea about business, about life as a whole.

Having experienced the power of a salesman's spirit, which this book will cultivate in you, you will also understand the power of being fully committed to what you are doing. Commitment, and in particular commitment to excellence, is such a powerful thing, that you will find me referring back to it many times throughout the book, it even has a full chapter dedicated entirely to it.

As time went by, I spent evenings, mornings and afternoons reading and listening to countless audio books, reading articles and blogs of authors from different countries and industries. Authors that all contributed to this immense knowledge and expertise.

Many times, the secrets and experiences discovered whilst using the accumulated knowledge never surfaced in a clear and understandable manner in any book written to this point. These were and still are very hard to describe and yet such influential points that noticing them and properly identifying them, still seems almost impossible. It takes one the knowledge of this book, to be able to work with those new discoveries on a daily basis. Not mentioning how much effort, it took me to put them all together expressively in text.

Since many ideas exposed in this book represent rare knowledge and newly discovered secrets in sales. In places were facts are not sufficient, it is explained with examples or short stories which will enable you to fully grasp the weight and the volume of every critical point you will encounter.

These will be facts on which I spent countless nights by trying to identify and put them in writing. Specifically in such a way that you can understand and benefit from them instantly. You can start applying those findings the moment you put in the extra effort and understand the idea behind each chapter.

As selling skills continued developing, and hard work gave a fresh understanding of the sales process. New ways to close transactions better & faster started surfacing, not only for products but also for personal skills and ideas to those you interacted with on a daily basis.

Since almost no Salesman from Middle East have studied the science of sales, new findings and evidence continued surfacing, that selling takes place in every part of our life even here. As such, observations continued, how young and old people sell their products to customers, and their ideas to friends and relatives.

Since every observations prompted me to approach and try to collect data, I started identifying new patterns of how people depended on whether they could present the idea successfully and explain the "features & benefits" to someone else professionally, just as a salesman does with his product.

I constantly point out that the commission in such cases it the approval and permission, or the action of buying into the idea. The commission is the convinced party doing what the convincing person wanted. Most of us have several important sales to make during our lifetime that influence our future. Learning to sell our ideas and ourselves is therefore the first thing every person must learn.

The first big sale we make is to the University, selling our achievements for a chance to enter the courses we desire. The commission is the chance to acquire knowledge and a certificate.

The second big sale is selling ourselves to a lovely partner that we would like to have in our life. We all want that partner to "Buy" into our vision and future plans with them. Our partners reward us with love, affection and commitment.

So the second sale is tougher than the previous one, here you must continually maintain the relationship with your partner. You have to give them at least the same and more in return every day if you want to get some "commission" in the form of love again. We build relationships according to these principles. We build any business around these principles of selling & persuading.

When contributing to each other, we are selling the idea that we can trust each other. By maintaining that trust, we are selling the idea that we can establish long-term goals together. As you can see, **selling is a very important skill that you must learn no matter what industry you are working in.**

Example:

To pursue your goal of becoming a worldwide renowned sales expert you must go to places where selling in the lifeblood of the country. After a quick research, let us say you determined you target as the UAE market. You applied and a world-renowned company recruited you, and they paid all the expenses to bring you to UAE. You successfully sold yourself as an expert with great personality, and unique skills. That company had no other choice but to offer you a good position in sales.

We attend an interview selling ourselves in exchange for a salary. The outcome is a result of how good we present our "features &

benefits" and weather the value we will bring into the company is higher than the "price", the salary Remember this, price is never an objection. Any company would pay any of us our dream salary, if we manage to convince them that we are the next Bill Gates or Steve Jobs. Every purchase involves risks, and you as a salesman are there to convince them that the risk is worth the result, and the results is worth more than the salary you ask for. It does not matter if you like selling or not, you are doing this on a daily basis. You should become great at it. Go through the entire book and become a professional, this will make you a millionaire in no time.

That first company I worked for was amazing; it had the perfect management team that encouraged me to pursue the goal of becoming part of the TOP salesman in the word. One of their main benefits was the amount of resources they offered all their employees. As I will later describe in this book, many of the employees who worked there were missing these resources, because they did not know how to identify and use those them. This crucial skill upon which you entire life depends, will be thoroughly discussed and explained in this book. This skill will push you up to the expert level, at which I am now! You should be here to, it feels so good, trust me!

In the first 6 months at this company I read, studied, and practiced in such amounts, that in the final month of employment there, before I switched to another incredible opportunity, I memorized and completed the entire induction for all management levels by myself without even my manager knowing it.

How did I do that? The company gave employees countless literature about customer relationship management, I opened the files that contained all the knowledge and started reading every day. These were accessible to anybody, so I studied them. I managed to complete this achievement because I always believed that your goals should be your dreams, not your quotas. Work on your goals daily, do whatever it takes, and then everything will be possible and within your grasp. If you really want something, you will find a way to do it no matter what.

Example:

Here in Middle East, a land of luxury and abundance with countless retail shops and the biggest malls on Planet Earth, with 50 degrees outside, rushing people to stay indoors all year long, combined with such an amount of air-conditioned shopping space, selling is a skill that dominates the atmosphere. Middle East is home to one of the most abundant retail markets, and I gathered all available knowledge and expressed it in this book.

If you want to get anywhere in selling, first get your skills at the right level by reading books and studying other successful people. Then, get to work in places abundant with sales like Middle East or any other economically strong region.

Another important treasure you will discover in this book is how you can use the company resources to develop yourself. You will amaze yourself by what those resources are when we start describing them. This book will initiate the greatest breakthrough in your career; this book will make you a professional!

The power gained by reading books is immeasurable. Reading books is an absolute necessity for you to succeed. In fact, reading this book from beginning to end is a commitment you must make and one of the greatest break troughs you will make in your career. "Stop Yelling Start Selling" has accumulated all the priceless and experiences from decades, and created a new way of thinking and understanding of a salesman's possibilities.

This book describes from zero to 101%, your career path towards becoming an absolute expert in Sales. All you must do is make a firm decision now to committing yourself to understanding every piece of information I have expressed in the chapters that will follow. I would wish you luck, but all you need is commitment to become the best!

How You Will Start Selling

Your decision to read and follow the guidelines in "Stop Yelling Start Selling" is one that you must take and commit as you begin.

Only then, you will change the course of your career dramatically. I personally congratulate you in bringing yourself up to the last step of evolution in the Sales Industry as a Sales Expert. By the time you will finalize reading this book you will acquire the following abilities:

- **You will learn how to dress** for catching the attention of your prospects or anyone else in your life. You will learn to sell yourself to your customer, as an expert in your industry, to your boss as an employee ready for a promotion, or successfully sell a product or service; everyone's eyes will be on you. Attention is the first step of any successful selling conversation. Dressing and attracting attention will be a start, but when it comes to attracting the right kind of attention and at the right intensity, that is already a true art and this book will tell you everything about it.

- **You will dramatically improve your body language** and learn that every movement coming from you will contribute either to the sales success or to its detriment. In any environment, no matter where you work nothing will distract the customer focus. At the same time, you will be able to understand your customer's non-verbal cues, which will inevitably boost your sales by knowing where you stand with them in regards to building trust, discussing their needs or pushing for the close.

- **Your voice, another factor this book will improve.** In the sales industry, the customer directs their attention at every pitch in your voice, which must be clear and will express double the meaning of any words coming out of your mouth. This book will help you communicate easily and confidently which will gradually pull even the angriest customer to your side. Your tone and speed of voice is a powerful weapon which when learned how to use properly, will become the extra edge so many Sales Executives miss out.

- **You will understand why you need to record your sales** process no matter how short. The book will give you all the necessary knowledge to and tools to determine which recording is more appropriate for your particular case depending on the environment, the customer, and your financial capabilities. You will even learn how to execute all of these with just a pen and paper, by knowing how to take notes and exactly what you need to note down.

- **You will learn to overcome the oldest challenge of them all.** Building effective customer relationships, and making a long lasting impression, which will win you not just a customer but also a friend. Your employers as you to talk about this subject during any sales interview; it is the bread and butter of any sales expert. In fact, building customer relationships quickly is the ultimate level of success. Salesmen speak about this so often, yet so few do it correctly. When done by the book, a customer will close the deal himself, or the close will be so easy that even a 7-year-old introverted child will master it.

- **You will learn how to close the sale and cash in that money**. At the end of the day, after all the effort you put into the relationship with your prospect, you success can only be measure by the amount of deals you have done. As my boss in Real Estate used to ask all the time "How many deals have you done this month?" a wise question giving birth to a cruel world if you are not prepared. Many of us do everything it takes to make the deal go through except the final step.

Here we will discuss how other salesmen subconsciously avoid closing because they are afraid to risk. They think they are still in the game because there is no definite answer as a yes or no, they think the sale is still going on just because they did not finalize it. What you will understand is that the game does not bring you money, the finish line of the game does. The close either gives you money or takes them away from you and your company. We tend to blame someone or something else for not closing the deal. We say the fault is the absence of a product the customer wanted. It will be the duty of this book to show that the fault of not closing a sale is always of the salesman. No matter what excuse you find, it was all in the salesman's hands at the end of the day. This book will give you the perfect solution for that as well.

- **Follow-up** is the magic of reconnecting with customers the right way. With those who have already purchased and those who are just potential buyers. If there is any single variable that would bring you back a customer when he has already departed from your store, it is your ability to follow up consistently. Bringing back and farming a customer that already exists is much easier and less expensive than gaining a new one. After all, the amount of people who want to buy your product is limited.

- **You will learn how to save your time**, health and money to do the right things first. A priceless thing called "time" which is constantly running out. In this book you will learn how to dominate and control it at work and when you go back home. We will discuss strategies to maximize your work/life balance in tough schedules that sometimes mean going home at 02.00 AM and starting work the same day at 06.00 AM. These strategies will not only increase you productivity the second day after a difficult shift, they will allow you to have more focus and time to dedicated to your spouse, kids and all who require your attention after work. Most of all, it will give you the ability to smile after a tough day and have a pleasant mood which will reflect on all your interactions with other people.

- **You will learn how to deal with nervous customers and co-workers at the same time.** I am constantly surprised how other authors never talk about this subject. While they should describe this subject together with everything that influence sales. Dealing with unpleasant moments is a vital skill, which will allow you to focus on the actual work, on the activity, or project you are working on. It will have a great impact on the attitude you have at work and how happy you are about it. Your attitude will always reflect on your customers and your ability to sell. This book will teach you how to stay up beat.

Every chapter has examples from the authors experience in the sales industry or a short story that will illustrate what theory cannot. These tools will define why the content that follows is important for you, what the main idea of it is and exactly how that knowledge reflects itself in practice. You will hear not only about the author's experiences, you will also hear about his colleagues who volunteered to share relevant stories that will help you better understand the contents of each chapter and use it to its full potential. The author however gave fictional name to the character of these stories.

This book is all for you. About what solutions you have, how you can maximize your sales, and how you should focus on closing your deals!

The Steps to Success

Since less is better, the structure of this book will make you get a tremendous benefit, from reading it from beginning to the end, or going directly to the area that you feel needs improvement and tackle it with the best techniques separately. After reading, your career progress and your sales will be enjoyable and as sweet as honey.

The internet and media is full of 10 things you have to and 20 things you should not. This book will give you not a list, but a path! It will give you the ability to become the #1 Sales Expert. You will have a clearly outlined path that you can follow from 0 to 101% and beyond. Since that is exactly what will guarantee you a perfect and flawless career!

The road to sales perfection starts here.

As mentioned before, fully read the book once first. Then, using the techniques described in it, asses the knowledge you have retained. You will get to know exactly what areas need improvement in your case.

When you understand that, open the book at the concerning chapter and make sure you implement the guide to get maximum results. So again, read the book fully once, and when you feel you are strong in all the chapters except one, go straight to it and work on eliminating that nasty thing which holds you back, because as practice has shown you are only as good as your worst performing skill.

Approach this challenge like a real hustler. You have to push through the end of the book to get the money you need.

How much time will it take you to become the #1 Retail Sales Expert"?

The short answer is, the moment you have understood and started following all the guides in this book, you will hear people around you says that you are the best, that you are a professional, that you know what you are doing. The moment that happens, you can truly consider yourself an expert of your craft.

The long answer is the following. The moment you even become the #1 Sales Expert in the world, you will blink and the next moment you are #2, and after 1 day, you are #1500. That will happen, if you do not continue improving and refining your skills. For this very important reason, the book does not give you just a solution to your problem; it teaches you in which way you can continuously develop your selling skills. When you go through the content presented here, make sure you do it more than once.

The first time you read, you will discover a new world. Everything is going to fall into its place. You will start recognizing you work environment as more structured, more familiar, you will understand the environment you work in like the back of your hand. This will generate new abilities as predicting what is going to happen both with your customer and with your colleagues. You will know exactly what will come next.

The first reading of the book will give you a solid foundation from which your career will start growing like the bamboo in tropics. Depending on how attentive and focused you will be during your first read, it will directly influence the amount of time it will take for you to set your foundation. Can you do it over night? Great, do you want to do it during a week or a month? Not a problem, but remember, as you lay your foundation you are investing your time. In addition, you can never start growing until you will lay a strong and solid foundation. You need solid ground to push, to shoot up like a rocket to the moon.

What happens next is only going to get more and more interesting. As you have finished reading, you will now have the book perfectly structured in your head. From then on, whatever happens in your career you come straight back to it and refer directly to the concerned chapter. That way, by the law of natural selection you will visit and read more often those chapters that are concerned with the issue you personally face at work.

Do you have problems communicating with customers? Fine, go to the necessary chapter.

You need advice on dealing with your boss. Excellent, we have a solution for you.

This book has been created by a salesman who perfectly knows what the daily challenges you face are. This book is the delivery of fresh experience straight from the battleground. There is nothing like it in the market, you mark my word on that. Any problem that you can possibly face in retail, you will find a solution to it in this book.

Get your engines ready to push! This book will add some gasoline to it, or if it sounds better to you, will load the first bullet into your sale gun.

Preparation is critical. As Churchill once said "The plan was nothing, but the planning was everything." I would add that in sales you have to close the sale no matter how much you planned for it. Close early and close often!

Now, let us teach you how to look, smell, talk and walk like the million-dollar person that you are.

At first, let us make it clear that you are not selling just your product; the real bonus your customer gets is you in the deal. You are the one that makes the difference between them signing or quitting. Your personality can convince them to buy!

Believing in yourself, and in your product, up to the point of being irrational is crucial. Learning to love sales and committing to excellence is the lifeblood of your career.

I can only tell you that preparation is truly the mark of a true professional!

How a Sale is Similar to The Work of a Craftsman

1.) **Construct the Sale**
2.) **Cut through Objections**

Construct the sale – During your sale conversation, it is important for you to understand how valuable every moment of the interaction is. Your strong points that manifest themselves in the first minutes of the conversation will influence the result of the sale.

That is right, constructing a sale is not a one-minute business and that is one of the first lessons.

Think about the sale as a smith thinks about creating a sword. First, he has to select the right kind of metals. Then, the smith combines these metals at the right temperature. More than that, it is very important for him to maintain a certain temperature to have a correct result. **"Strike the iron while it is hot"**.

The same way you, as a professional salesman, begin the process of constructing your conversation. You gather prospects and make sure your pipeline is full. Than you filter out the prospects that are worthy of spending your time with from the ones that are just browsing, just as the smith is selecting the right kind of metal for his sword. After you have filtered out the weeds, you start building temperature and putting it all together. You start communicating, but you do not just throw anything at you prospect to make a sound. You have to be careful, one word more or one word less and the temperature of your conversation will be off balance and your sword, or your sale might fail.

The moment your temperature is right and the customer has warmed up to you. Strike the iron by asking questions. This way you are giving shape to your conversation and you are giving it direction, just as the smith gives shape to his sword. More and more as you go, with every successful strike, which should be your questions; you will start seeing a shape coming out. You will start understanding exactly what your customers' needs are. To put it in other words, you will know where the sword needs adjustments. Depending on the type of prospect you have, constructing the sale could take from minutes to hours or even days.

That is why making sure everything involved is worthy of your time, is just as important as it is for the smith, making sure he will not waste his efforts on the wrong materials. To do that, understand if you customers have the money and power to make the decision of buying your product. If not, find out whom those people are and make them join the conversation before you move forward.

To know when you prospect lights up in green as "qualified", you have to keep in mind what the goal of the conversation is before you even start it, and what answers you are looking for. You have to visualize what the result of you sales will look like, as the smith can visualize exactly how his sword will look.

Cut through objections – After you finished building the customer relationship, you have to start pushing for the sale. You will accurately push your customer to the edge of closing. With every brush of words you put in, you have to get one-step closer to closing the sale. When you will learn how to push them to the edge smoothly and quickly, your sale will be a masterpiece.

You will cut through objections and complaints just as fast and as effective as a sword of an expert smith cuts through anything. Your sword will make the difference between winning and losing a war. **You conversation will make the difference between selling and going home conquered of having conquered.**

Commitment to Excellence

The first thing you must understand and engrave in your mind, you have to commit to being excellent. You must decide now, that you will be excellent in everything done by you. Excellence means you will give 100% percent of everything you have. Your last thought, breath and movement should be in the direction of your goals.

We will break down the commitment to excellence in several pieces:

1. **Fight to Dominate your market**
2. **Bite More than you can chew**
3. **Become Excellent in taking risks**
4. **Get to the point of No Return**
5. **You are in People's business**
6. **Be Obsessed with success**

Fight to Dominate your market - In this world staying competitive is not what you are looking for. I remember how at the university they used to teach us that competition is good for the markets and that competition makes everyone perform at high levels. Well listen carefully now, competition is good in a perfect and theoretical world only. **If you want to have any chance of gathering the first million or billion soon, you have to dominate your market.** You have to be an absolute relentless beast, the beast of the zoo. You have to be the hunter and everyone else has to be your deer. You will achieve domination only with such an attitude.

Look at big corporations like Microsoft, Apple, Unilever, they dominate the market and continue expanding and dominating every single hour. They will buy another company from its roots if that is what it will take to help them maintain their status. Governments have 100% domination over their territories, these mechanisms are the ultimate and most complicated organizations in the world and their goal is to dominate. The governments and corporations will never accept the status quo; they continue pushing to eliminate every possible competition in their way. They will never accept someone competing for their core values as Territory, Economy or even Traditions. At the same time, we all know what happens to companies that compete against the government.

You need to become as fearless and as effective as those who dominate your current market and eliminate any competition immediately. Take example from governments that go against each other. The moment they threaten each other's possibilities to dominance over their territory, a war or a battle is inevitable, physically and economically.

What is war you may ask?

It is an active battle that has claimed more than about 1000 people. Has the world ever seen time of peace? For the last 6.000 years, we have been entirely at peace for 120 of them, or just 2 percent of recorded history. 108 million have died in the twentieth century. Estimates for the total number killed in wars throughout all of human history range up to 1 billion. Governments kill people to defend their beliefs, companies will cut jobs by thousands leaving people with no food and income. **That is how cruel the world you are living in is.**

If you are not willing to put effort into being the best in your industry by getting excellent at what you do, there is no place for wealth and prosperity in your life.

This world is built around people and organizations that know what they do, and do it excellently. They do it so well that nobody else can get even close to their results. They make sure to maintain that status by constantly improving their skills, by constantly scouting for new strengths, weaknesses and opportunities. They are committed to excellence!

They know, if they have even one flaw, their competitor will immediately find ways to exploit it. If you wish to perform in an excellent manner, dominate your territory. You cannot afford to have any mistake or any drawbacks, in any aspect that affects your goals.

Excellence is not a choice anymore; it is a standard required to be at the top of the league. If you ever hope to exit the middle class, which is getting poorer and poorer by every year, you have to dedicate yourself to becoming excellent in selling, excellent at grooming, excellent in building customer relationships, excellent in closing the sale and all other things presented in this book.

Bite more than you can chew - Another way in which you can secure your commitment to excellence, is by constantly pushing for more than you think you need. Notice how the word *"think" is used*. Experience shows that we will always need more the moment we achieve it. So why should not you create a bigger target from the start? Why increase your target every time you achieve a small goal, when you can set a big target and become motivated by the importance of achieving it. Go for a greater milestone towards making your dreams come true. Simply put, multiply your target with a number. This is an unbelievably effective technique used by the top performers in any industry.

Any plan is likely to fail when it encounters reality, consequently it is impossible to calculate and plan for all events, unless you multiply your target. In that case, you will always be sure to hit the initial goal you set if you really shoot for a greater one.

Your problems will change; small issues will not distract you anymore. Whichever number you pick for the multiplication, make sure you achieve your new goal in the same period. It is very important for you to achieve all your targets when you set them initially, so that your "number" starts building up reputation.

Get in the habit of achieving what you put your mind to when multiplying your target. Achieve that goal no matter what. If you multiplied your target by say 20 and all you have achieved is 90% from that, you have to push to the end no matter what. If you have to go out with your friends, cancel it, if your phone is ringing do not answer.

Are you hearing this? **You will never be able to achieve such high targets that are 10 or 20 times greater than your initial goal if anything in the process distracts you.**

This is exactly the reason for using such a *"hack"* if you wish to call it. You put yourself into a positively stressful situation, which will make you do your absolute best in achieving your goal. You no longer have the entire day to sell one car, you have 10 hours left to sell 10 cars and the clock is ticking, your problems changed. You cannot waste even one minute because you might have several hours without a sale.

Listen to what I am about to say carefully! **Take your target seriously and do not allow anything to distract you.** If you can do this, a miracle will happen. Yes, something divine. You will see how your mind starts becoming creative and starts racing to find new solutions. You will start doing things that you have never done before because you will have problems that you never had before. You will be in a state where people around you will look like they are turtles merely walking around and you are the rabbit, which wants to go even faster. If you want to achieve your target within the deadlines, you must get out of your skin, get out of your comfort zone and find a way to do it.

Example:

Not having credit on your telephone will no longer be an excuse; you will find a way to call your customer no matter what. Those prospects that you were calling casually to maintain a relationship with, they will be your best chance of achieving your target. When you will call them, nothing will be able to distract, no sound and no notification. You will listen and understand every word that comes out of your customers' mouth. You will ask questions, and then ask even more questions, because you will be hungry for success. At that moment you will experience such confidence in your product, you will either make that customer buy or walk out of the store asking himself "Who was that guy?" That is because you will push them to decide in your favor no matter what. Your confidence will be irrational because you have a goal that you must hit no matter what.

Where will all of these thoughts and attitude come from? **Just like a beast chased into a corner, you will have no other choice but to attack, there will be no more place for stepping back, this is exactly why you will find a way to make that sale.**

After some time, multiplying your goals will give you confidence in your ability to complete them, because you have done it so many times. Since you have achieved the goals before, you will know that doing whatever you put your mind to, is perfectly possible. At that moment, you have cracked the code of success! That blissful moment when everything will start seeming possible is the ultimate breakthrough on your way to becoming rich beyond your wildest dreams!

With this attitude, the possibilities are endless. Research shows we are using only 2% of our brain, yes not even 10%; you use just 2% to accomplish our daily tasks. Imagine how great your potential is and how easy it is to miss that immense advantage if you do not have the right attitude, the right plan and the right goals.

Always, always push to achieve your goals. That way, the next time you set a goal, you will automatically have confidence in your potential to achieve it. I cannot stress this enough: **The potential that you have within your self is limitless if you only choose to exercise it.** There is no limit to what you can achieve, because even after you do calculate your limit, you will break through it by simply being committed to excellence. That is the ultimate mark of biting more than you can chew and then chewing it.

Become excellent by taking risks - Excellence does not mean staying away from failures. Excellence means that knowing what you now know, you will make the best choice possible and implement all the resources that you can to achieve your target. Being a risk taker gives you the extra edge you need to get ahead of others who are simply good at calculating, estimating and playing it safe. Taking risks will give you the ability to implement and fail, repeatedly without giving up, to the moment that you become perfect in taking calculated risks. Excellence in taking risks is the willingness to make a calculated decision, which might bring losses & profits to your company. However, the profits must be greater and have a higher chance of taking place.

Example:

If you have 100% of gaining 1 million, and 50% of gaining 100 million, you will go for the second, because 100 million times 50% is much more than 1 million times 100%. If this sounds like something interesting for you to research, the name is "The Game Theory".

What better example than a risk-taking salesman, who will shake of anyone's doubts, by confidently pushing them to purchase while knowing the buyer might get angry at such kind of aggressive tactics. Surely you have meat at least one person like that in your life.

Try to remember the time when someone came along and everything around worked the way they wanted it to. They were moving effortlessly among all the noise around them. On the other hand, maybe even you had one of those moments when you felt that you are the boss and no one can shake your authority no matter what. You were the king of the mountain and everything was possible for you, you were willing to take any risks and you were sure about the result. Or those amazing girls you found uncomfortable talking with before, when you feel like the boss, they are the ones who have to look away and blush while you just stand there looking and realizing how great you are. Alternatively, remember those super rich customers who you were so afraid to spoil the relationship with if you push them to buy. Now your flow was priceless and you have managed to convince them and push them to take even more.

These are blissful moments, when they go away you are like, "Wow, what did just happen to me? How did I do that?" Those are times of you being a true risk taker and confidence is synonymous with you.

That state of mind achieved regularly is the mark of a charismatic individual; it is like an aura that revolves around you influencing everything with what you interact. That is how you achieve excellence. Nothing less than those kind of moments will bring you total domination over your competition.

Get to the point of No Return - The greatest people on earth, use a principle called the point of no return. It is the point, beyond which you must continue working on your current goals because turning back is impossible. Many great generals have used this principle to win wars and change the course of history.

After their entire army debarks the ships, they order to set them on fire, sending a clear message to everyone: We Win or We Die. When people face only these two alternatives, you can expect them to perform at 101% of their potential. They will reach heights they thought they never would, excellence will no longer be an option, and it will be a standard. Because if they do not achieve excellence they will die, for whatever that means in their case.

Take the invaluable knowledge that great generals applied for thousands of years to conquer new territories and use it for conquering your dreams. **Do not leave yourself a way back; do not give yourself a second chance. Make your decisions and stick to them in such a way that going back is crazy. There should be nothing in the world that will make you give up!**

Example:

I use the same principle while writing now. I use this principle every single time. I set goals, break them down and execute the next action while making the desired result public. I leave no way for going back. I burn all ships and bridges; the only important thing now is to push aggressively for completing the goals. After announcing publicly my intentions, both my reputation and my EGO are at stake. In addition, I bet you 101% that I will achieve those goals! You can learn how to do all of it yourself, by going through the entire book and being committed to practice what you learn.

Commit to being excellent at achieving your goals. Eliminate any possibilities of you giving up on them. If you have to announce it publicly, do it. Tell everyone that you are going to be a huge embarrassment if you do not achieve those goals. Remember the example of how great generals applied this principle. They burned their ships and sent out a clear message to their entire army that winning is the only option. You must adopt the same way of thinking. Do not leave yourself a way back for "plan B" if you want "plan A" to succeed. You will amaze yourself by what potential you have, when there is no other choice but to win!

We are here to achieve greatness, to be excellent in sales. We are here to get our millions & the sooner the better. Make excuses vanish! No more distractions, nothing matters more than achieving your goal and maintaining your reputation.

These false alibis about why you cannot do it, kill every action that you can actually take. It is a justification your mind creates to keep you from wasting energy.

The human being has evolved to save energy; it will always tend to do less. Our body does not know if what we are doing now is worth the energy. It constantly keeps pushing to get more rest. Life does not work that way. If you want results, start doing and take action!

You can only be great after you decide to use 101% of your potential. Stop coming up with reasons for being lazy; start finding reasons for taking action.

Do not let your mind grow soft. That is the greatest enemy you have after you achieve something. Do not take the rest you have earned, take the money and go get more! Stop settling for what you have & accepting being part of the middle class. All these excuses will eventually kill your dreams and goals if you allow them too far. Make it a habit of hating excuses, go out there and hunt them down, challenge them!

When I hear the inner voice trying to convince me of postponing something for tomorrow. I cannot resist the temptation of punching that excuse in the face by taking immediate action. That is right. The only Remedy for excuses and procrastination is immediate action. You do not need to think about it another minute. What you need to do is get up now an immediately take action.

It is amazing how many people have the skills, the knowledge, the resources and possibilities to achieve their goals. Yet when it comes to taking action, they decide to stay in their comfort zone. They think, because they have all the resources: they can do it tomorrow; they can do it the next week, the next year ... and then end up doing it 10 years later or never at all.

People must remember that the scarcest resource they have in this life is time. We will never have enough of it. We can use it more productively, yet no matter if we are or if we are not, time is running out. The fewer things we accomplish, the more time we throw away with our own hands. **We literally take huge chunks of our time and throw them off the cliff into nowhere.**

While I sit here writing and knowing that the goal I just set is nearly impossible. Every second that goes by is priceless. I know that one-minute too late and I might not make it. I know that there still is chance of achieving my goal, and that small chance is driving my performance to the limits. Commitment to excellence is what drives my attitude now; commitment to excellence is what will bring you great results.

You are in People's business - Excellence for a salesman is about understanding that You Are in the selling business and you also are in the people's business. How many of you know sales experts that are incredibly good at pushing and shoving the products down the throat of a customer that even they do not believe in. Not many I believe. These people can only be average, they are never great, and they are never excellent at what they are doing. The highest they can go up to is be the kings of average.

Now remember that time when you met a great salesman or heard a speech of a great salesman on the internet. Remember how their passion filled you with enthusiasm; remember how they really cared about people. That is exactly what lures their audience to come to their presentations repeatedly. Those sales experts know that they are in the people's business. They know, even though there are many sales and closing techniques around every corner, the human being is so complex, that if the real reason behind all of your skills is not sincerity, genuine interest and commitment to solve their problems, everything else will have superficial results.

Books teach you skills & strategies you can use at work. However, books cannot decide for you to commit in using the skills you have learned.

Commit to helping people and understand that they pay you money to resolve their problems. When you will have absolute confidence and 101% commitment to excellence, people will rain money over you.

The moment your prospect will feel that the driving force behind all of your skills and expertise is the genuine idea of helping make this world a better place, they will give you all their money. Money will come running out of their pocket towards you themselves.

We are all looking for solutions that can change our lives for the better. We are all ready to pay huge amounts of money, if that will bring us much more in return. I will borrow a million today if I was 100% sure I can invest and get 101% at least out of it, wouldn't you?

Be smart; surround yourself with those kind of products and services that are a solution, not a burden. Learn about them and prove to yourself how great they are. Sell yourself on your products and you will automatically offer your customers excellent solutions.

Be Obsessed with success - Excellence is nothing less off becoming obsessed with success. Become overwhelmed by the idea of achieving your goals, to the point that people around you cannot ignore this fact. Let them say you are irrational, because that is exactly what you should be. **Normal is average, and the average person on this planet is poor and starving.**

The total wealth of the richest 1% will overtake that of the other 99 percent of people in 2016, unless someone will correct the current trend of rising inequality. If you are reading this after 2016, check where these trends currently are.

Read that again!

Off course, you have to be obsessed, off course you have to be crazy about achieving what you need to achieve. Off course, only obsession will drive you to being excellent.

Do you know what happens, the moment you are not obsessed with something? You will be distracted! Something else will occupy space in your mind and pump up its importance in front of your eyes; because you are not motivated enough, to keep doing what you should in order to achieve your goals. Sure, you are interested, sure, you want to get it done, but obsession is what removes any distraction.

To illustrate this better, I urge you to do the following exercise. Hold your breath naturally for a longer time until you feel how it simply becomes uncomfortable. In this moment, all you care about is getting more oxygen. There is nothing in the world that can convince you from stopping to breathe and directing your attention at something else. There are no exceptions, there are no rules, and there are no limits to the extent that you are going to go to get more air. Because going back is impossible, you have burned all our ships, there is no plan B, if you stop breathing, you will die. Remember this feeling well and train yourself to project it on your goals!

Understand that life is about achieving your goals; there is nothing more important than that. Your ultimate goal is to be happy. If you are in sales, this means closing more deals, getting more cake and having a happy family while being financially secured. If you want to get there, you have to commit to excellence. Because you are not the only one who wants that on planet earth. There are billions of people around the globe competing with you for the same right now.

Right now, this very moment, billions of people are working on being better than you are! When you are on the couch watching TV instead of reading a book to improve your skills, billions of people are improving theirs. When you are sleeping, billions are practicing. When you are eating, playing computer games, no matter if you are doing something towards or against your goals, everyone else is busy working on their dreams. You can only become one of the TOP performing salesman by being obsessed with your craft.

In fact, let me say it to you now, you will not be normal when you conquer your goals, you will be a champion, you will be a warrior obsessed with winning. You are going to have enthusiasm, charisma, and the reflexes of going 101% in everything you do.

Become obsessed with excellence and nothing shorter than that!

Take Action Daily

From experience, I could tell: When it comes to results, action is the root of them all. Taking massive action generates massive results. Which in turn equals an accumulation of great experience that eventually turns into gigantic profits.

This chapter is composed from the following points:

1.) Failure is an Event, Success is a Results
2.) Take action NOW, as you read
3.) Consistency is not just a word

Failure is an event, success is a result - It does not matter if you fail at one action you take or all of them. As long as you keep pushing and keep coming up every time you fall down, failure will not be a result, it will be a part of your path to success. You must continually push and take massive amount of action no matter what. Look, getting to where I am now did not happen by lying down on a couch. I took incredible amount of constant action for the past two years to get where I am now. What was the result? I received daily calls from companies asking me to come work for them. It was I interviewing the company now, not vice versa.

People told me that after trying everything, I will become tired and quit. Because that is what happened to them, they will try convincing others not to try. So why didn't I quit so far? Why did I refuse to accept that "I could not do it" whenever I failed? What attitude pushed me to get back up, to succeed every time I failed? **It was the genuine belief that if others who have 24 hours a day could do it, I can do it as well.**

How can someone live with the idea of failing and giving up without ever trying succeeding one more time? Whenever I come across these kind of people, the moment I understand that I have these kind of people in my circles, I get rid of them!

That is right, run from them like the U.S. citizens run from EBOLA or the Middle East runs from MERS. These people are like a virus; their negativity is infecting everything around them. I am sure you have met them yourself in this life and can relate to this. You have to surround yourself with positive likeminded people. With energetic people who are just as goal oriented as you. People live with successful habits as part of their lives. You know what they say: Surround yourself with nine millionaires and your will be the tenth.

Take such amount of massive actions that people will start telling you: "Hey brother, you are too pushy, that is too invasive. You are trying too hard". Most important thing, you need to hear that from top performers, not lazy people in your circles. That is how hard you have to focus on taking action.

Example:

Have a look at how my morning starts. I wake up 2 hours before work. What do I manage in this time? I do a 10-minute exercise routine to wake up and keep the blood flow energetic. I than take a shower and get dressed. For the remaining 1 hour, I sit down to work 30 minutes on this book and 30 minutes before work I am out of the house. Could I have done something else in those 30 minutes instead of writing this book? Yes, I could! Could I have just set on the couch or checked my Email or Facebook? Yes, I could. In fact, 30 minutes might even turn out as not being enough for those activities. Therefore, instead of wasting time, I sit down and work on current goals, because I have them right in front. I stay motivated by pushing myself to achieve those goals in the timeframe I gave myself before. I do what I put my mind to and I leave no way back!

Look, as soon as you announce that you are going to shoot for the stars, you will have people telling you: "The slower you go the further you get." and all that kind of unproductive stuff. Get rid of them; get rid of those people now! Those people gave up on their dreams; those people do not believe in themselves no more. They decided, since the world demands too much action for them to breakthrough, they are better off sitting down & doing nothing. Get away from them. Surround yourself with nine millionaires and you will be the tenth.

When taking action, remember: The more you do it, the better it is. The less you do it, the worse it gets. To do that, you have to learn how to structure your time throughout the day. You need to work all the time you work, and sleep all the time you sleep. Look, taking action is not only necessary to become a sales expert; you need to take action in all aspects of your life. If you want to be successful at improving your selling skills or anything else, like have a great family, **take action!**

Let me ask you one thing, about action. Did you ever come to work late? If yes, how do you plan on growing your kids and supporting your family if you cannot make it in time to work? All it takes you is to get out of the house early! That is everything it takes! You think those 30 minutes of sleep have greater influence on your life than your reputation at work as "The guy who's always late."

If you really want to become the #1 sales expert in your field, you have to be willing to give up sleep and take action. **Not mentioning you have to plan your day before, so that you actually have enough sleep at the end of the day.** However, if you are late for work, you probably do not do that. If you do, make a realistic plan. Create it out of bullet points, which will guide you to the achievements of your daily goals. Follow through it. Do the most important things first. Take incredible amounts of action, stop trying one or two things and quitting if these do not work.

Look, you can never succeed if you give up after a few tries. In fact, you can only take massive amounts of actions by deciding that you will not give up. You should simply never give up and continue taking action until you succeed.

Take action NOW, as you read – We will take action together now! By the end of this chapter, we are going to have written down three most important tasks that you must accomplish on a daily basis. We will keep in mind your life goals. Your daily tasks will bring you closer to your goals every time you accomplish them. We will crush the idea of unachievable dreams and we will start working on them immediately.

First, we have to do the following:

1. Take something where you can write a note and make sure that note will be in front of your face all of the time. This means if you are on your way to work you can check these notes, when you are at home, at work or at the gym, you must be able to check on these notes. Consequently, the best idea would be to write them down in your smart phone. If you do not have a smartphone, get one, because this book will teach you how to become a millionaire with it.

2. Write down the number "24". Twenty-four, is the total amount of hours you have per day. Subtract from those eight hours of sleep. Than minus your work hours on a regular day, and hours you spend on transportation to work. All that you have left now is time you spend with your family, and time for self-improvement! Most of you have about 5 to 3 hours left. If you have more than that, you had better invest some of those into developing yourself friend! **Make sure your engines push you in the right direction every day! Reading this book is definitely one of the activities that you must do, if you want to become successful in selling and in life.**

3. Now that you know how much time, you have on a daily basis; work on your personal dreams. Write down what you current biggest goal in life is. It should be big and complementary to your dreams and aspirations.

4. Find out 3 to 10 tasks that you must complete for achieving your goal. After you complete those tasks, you should achieve your goal or have it at an arm's reach. Find out what those tasks are. If any of them will seem too vague or complicated, break it down again into another 5 to 10 even smaller tasks.

5. Give every task a priority by writing in front of it an "A" "B" "C" or "D", "A" being the TOP priority. Things that require your daily attention must be marked as priority level "A". These are routines like reading this book, working on your online popularity as an expert in your industry so on and so forth. Your career as a salesman is very dependent on these goals. Start your day with them and continue working through other "A" tasks that are on your list. An "A" grade tasks is something that you must accomplish before a "B" grade task. You will never touch a "B" task, unless all you are "A" tasks are completed. This is the ultimate weapon of achieving great results!

6. Take Action, Go Get It! – You heard it, Go Get It! Put all of these in your phone, in your locker, at your work desk, set it as your wallpaper for your PC or smartphone and start hustling for it! Train yourself to want it so bad that you are ready to die for it! Start working on them in the order of their priority! Re read your goals every time you wake up and go to bed, so that you stay on track with where you are going.

Going through these points, is the most powerful way in which you will take massive amounts of action. Nevertheless, remember it is all in the doing not the thinking! Reading about it here is the first part, implementing it is the second and most important part. You need both to gain results!

Get your attitude and everything around you in the "Do It" state. Taking this forward will be a piece of cake. Discipline yourself to take action DAILY and in an organized manner.

There is never enough time to do everything you have to. You will go to sleep today without having accomplished many things that you should have. Isn't it better to leave unaccomplished "Cs" that are less important, than lose the possibility of accomplishing "As" which are the most important ones? Wouldn't it be logical to end your day, having finalized goals that bring you the most of results? Sure, it would.

This is so important that I will repeat it again: Get yourself a notebook or a task manager on your phone. Put that task manager right in front of your face. Let it be the first thing that pops up when you turn on your device make it the home screen.

Example:

My phone has the home screen transformed into a daily planner. Here I have "A" priority tasks, which "I" must accomplish on a daily basis, "B" priority tasks and "C" priority tasks.

My "As" are so demanding that sometimes it might take me a whole day to complete one of them. I do not play with small goals; I want excellence and nothing less in this life. That is why I set my target high. Bite more than you can chew and then chew it!

Consistency is not just a word - or an action. Consistency is about becoming so daily that it is already part of your lifestyle. You have to breathe it, you have to eat it, and you have to dream it. Consistency is Daily Action. Consistency means you waking up in the morning, before the alarm, because you know there are things to accomplish and you do not have the luxury of endless time.

Consistency is to keep working and remembering that you have burned all your ships and there is no way back. It is when you get to the point of asking yourself: "Why am I rushing anywhere if I can just give myself one more day?" and then reminding yourself how important it is to achieve your goals. Than get straight, back into it!

Consistency means putting your money where your mouth is. This is applicable not only for your goals but also most importantly in your sales. As I will mention many times in this book, you can never hope to achieve excellence without being obsessed with what you are doing. If you are obsessed about selling that product than go ahead and prove that. Buy it and be proud with owning a piece. Take action! It does not matter if it is too expensive; everything is too expensive these days. That is why we have a bank to borrow money.

You might suggest that I am crazy, recommending you to use your credit card for buying the product you are selling. I am not crazy, I know that you have to be obsessed with your product if I want to convince someone to buy it.

When your customer will come in, 90% of them, they will be in the same position as you are currently convincing yourself of being. They are without money, with a bunch of problems and on a budget. So hey, guess what, if you could not convince yourself about buying what you are selling, a person that you know for a lifetime. You can never hope of convincing someone else about it who you just met. Show your customer that you are consistent, that you have already done what you are advising them to do. Tell them how you also took this hard decision before, and how worthy the product turned out to be. How it changed your life and how it continues to contribute to the comfort of your life on a daily basis. You will never be able to pull that off, unless you believe in your product to the point of purchasing and using it yourself.

Consistency in taking action is also about being smart. Think of a time when you will want to give up, than think of a way to outsmart your lazy self. Find some way to reward yourself and push your limits at the right moment. Stay on track with your plan of getting what you want, refuse to be left behind.

Example:

Let others know publicly what you are working on and what you would like to achieve. Let everyone know about your goals and the timeframe you give yourself to achieve them. This will put you in a point of no return. You will either have to do what you said you are going to, or risk looking as a failure in front of everyone who saw your announcement.

Too many of us these days make up some New Year resolutions that die the second day or week. Because there is no value built around them, there is no reason for commitment or the commitment is so weak that it takes a minimal distraction to shake them off the course.

If you want to achieve excellence and obtain great results, you have to have that little extra which not everyone else does. You have to be different. Knowing where other people do mistakes you must use that information to your benefit and take cation in those directions.

Someone who scores seven out of 10 daily easily beats someone who scores 10 out of 10 once a year. Being consistent in what you do is one of the keys to success in sales. The successful salesmen in this world perfectly understand this concept. It is one of the fundamental reasons how they have achieved great results. Professional salesmen look at their daily achievements as a bigger picture. They know that consistency is a gold mine, and they will keep taking daily action towards mining it.

Professional salesmen remind themselves daily: "Hey, it's time to go back and get some more. Because if I will not, there are another 7 billion people that will and I will be left behind by all of them." These kind of thoughts represent a commitment to consistency in the work you do. These kind of thoughts will ensure that you take action on a daily basis!

You are a high quality, smart and successful person with amazing opportunities waiting for you. Opportunities will come to you at any time and many times. This is why you have to prepare yourself for them every day. You have to consistently perform and overachieve. Consistently look for problems and find solutions.

All of this is true and fabulous, but how do you get it done? The biggest advice is this:

Write down your goals; make sure they are in front of your eyes on a daily basis. No dream can come true without first materializing itself on "paper". That is the true commitment to taking action! Do it now!

To Sell - Love Selling

Everything you do, at one point, will have a sale involved. That is a fact and that it is inevitable. Every action we do on a daily basis involves one sale at least. The first sale you make is you sell yourself on the necessity to take that action.

In this chapter, we will understand the following points:

    1.) Selling is a Good Thing When Done the Right Way
    2.) Selling Techniques are the Same, Markets Change

Selling is a Good thing when done the Right Way - Either you sell yourself to your boss, your spouse or you sell your product to the customers, you will make a sale today. Because sales is important no matter where you work, you must learn to sell everything that brings revenue to your company, and learn to do it the right way.

Is it a service? Is it a product? Both ways, you need to find your prospects and give them good business. You had better do that with skills and class. Do you hear this? Selling is the avenue of revenue! You will not earn money, if nobody wants to buy anything from you! Learn to love sales and life will treat you like a King!

The number one thing you have to learn is how to sell. Now some of you will say, "Andrei I am not a sales man, I did college at the Harvard or XYZ University and I do not consider myself a sales man. My mom used to tell salesmen are the poorest people, because she used to discriminate every salesman that entered our house. "

Well guess what, she discriminated them because they were bringing something she needed and were taking money in return. Most importantly those were unprofessional salesman who did not know what they are doing, that is why you mother or father does

not have respect for them. Nobody likes giving away money, so off course few salesman can come across a likable.

The difference though between salesman and sales professionals, is that the later give more benefits and more service, so the customer receives more than he pays. The point is the following. At the end of the day, the person who is selling is the one that goes home with the money for the product and the extra premium to putt in his own pocket. Do you want to be that person? Do you want to be on the side of people who cash in more than they spend? Learn to love sales and become and expert at it!

I remember hearing someone tell, "Those salesmen are pushy liars." Nothing could be further from the truth!

A professional salesman is someone who is so convinced that his product is the best solution to your problems that he might even come across as pushy or invasive. I will explain to you why that happens now and why every professional salesman should be pushy.

When you go to a luxury fashion store and you want to buy a suit or a dress, you know what you are approximately looking for. Than the salesman comes along and starts asking you questions. He asks you what are your preferences, what will you style it with, what colors you like, what are the other guests going to wear if you are attending an event, or what Is the dress code. Then, only then, he will offer you a personalized advice. You might not like that advice, which is what generally happens most of the time. However, the real professional will continue pushing you to take it. Do you think that too aggressive? Not at all, a professional will be pushing you to purchase because he is an expert at what he does, he finds out what are your problems, and he wants you to have the solution. He is pushy because he understands the product; he looks at it every day. Therefore, when he hears your needs he is sure that you are going to benefit from it and that would be your best choice.

Keep in mind. The only people who will get upset on a salesman are those who are not yet convinced that what he is offering is the right thing for them. Therefore, as a salesman, your job is to sell yourself on the product. No matter how much you know about your product, it will take an incredible amount of passion to convince someone that what they did not like initially, is actually, what they should buy for their own good.

Passion is a viral thing, because it spreads like a plague. So easily, that it can overpass your customer's logic and shoot straight at their heart. When you can play such a deep game with your boss, spouse and your customer, you will be able to sell them anything including your skills, knowledge and expertise. This mindset is what is going to bring you up to the next level in sales. Success will only be a question of time!

Example:

How people get upset on things they do not understand. I remember watching once a group of people singing and dancing on the streets of Netherlands, back when I was studying there at the University. They were making some kind of strange rituals and they looked like members of a Rugby club. I can also recall how I immediately became judgmental of them and simply started discrediting their action and hating whatever they did. They looked so disorganized, so careless. Moreover, suddenly it hit me. I asked myself "Why do I hate them, is it because I do not understand what they are doing? Is it because I am not sold on their idea as they are?" Therefore, I put myself right there in the situation of trying to figure out why this happened.

"Ok, so what do I understand about them? What can I recognize in their actions? I can see they are committed, they do not disturb anyone, they are all on the same page, they all have the same idea and all of them cheer and idolize the same person by dancing around him.

They look like having a great bunch of fun and laughs. That is actually so cool!"

That moment I realized, even if others might say, "Look at those... and look at what they are doing..." what about themselves? The ones that are criticizing, what are they doing? They have no spirit; they just sit around and do nothing to raise the morals of the society. Nothing to cheer people up or get people to look at them with interest like this Rugby club did, because they sure got my attention.

Therefore, before you start selling whatever you have to. Quit making bad comments about it and thinking it is a bad product. Get on the side of people who love it, ask them why they love it and understand how it helps them. Than use the same ideas and motive to point out to others why they will love the product and why they absolutely have to own it.

Selling techniques are the same, Markets Change - The principles of sales will stay the same as they were before. What does change is the market where the sales occur, the products and the communication channels. For example, hundreds of years ago when you went out to buy some cheese, you knew straight away what type of cheese you wanted because you have been eating it for the past 3 years. You wanted the same color, the same consistency and the same smell. Therefore, when you went to the market and someone had white cheese, while you wanted yellow, you were not going to buy it.

What happens in our days however is very different. You go online and research the cheese you want to buy, you search for some tips on what kind of cheese will go best with your pasta and you read the description of its smell. You start wondering: "Hmmm will it smell the way I think or different?" Therefore, you go to the store to have a look.

When you enter the store, you have your credit card in your pocket, you have your mind set to buy, and you are shaking from all sides and pieces because you know that you want. Everything is set for you to make a purchase...

Nevertheless, imagine the sales associate does not even come up to you. Imagine she does not even acknowledge that you came in. That store will lose a sale because the sales associate does not love selling.

Now let us say that she did end up servicing you well, she came along and asked you how is your day, she started a nice conversation with you and took it in the direction of what you are looking for. You told here everything you found out online and she points out to you two different types of cheese. They match your requirement exactly. She also tells you that switching between the two will not get you bored. What do you do? You end up buying both of them.

That is the mindset you should have as a sales executive. The person it not just looking for cheese, the person is looking to buy something more like your good service, the commodity of not getting bored. This is the consumer mindset of the 21st century. This is just one of the opportunities that you can have by being proactive. Do not just offer what the prospect wants; arouse needs that they never knew existed. How do you do that? By selling yourself on your product and then selling it to everyone else, you encounter.

Understand that selling is not just a job but also a great responsibility. You can accomplishing someone's dream no matter what your product is. If the customer wants what you have, this means it is part of their dreams and goals to have it. Now you have in your own hands the power to satisfy those needs. **All you have to do is help them understand exactly why your product is fit for fulfilling those desires and why they should buy it from you.**

Throughout history, selling has become a job that people are not very proud of attending. Media publishes the image of a greedy and lying salesman repeatedly. A person defrauding others to get their money, or a product that actually does not do what it has to do. Those people and products do not represent the true professional salesman. **People who cheat are not salesman. People who cheat are amateurs.**

People who resort to fraudulent tactics are not smart enough to pick a company that has worthy products in the first place. In addition, even if the products they sell are worthy, they are so mediocre that they cannot distinguish between people who do and do not need them. They push it to everyone including those who have absolutely no necessity for it. Those amateurs not only lie to their customers but also ruin the reputation of this profession. They ruin the reputation of their company. They are creating a negative image about the entire industry all over the world. Most of all, they never reach to the potential income they could have, if they simply improved their skills.

Think about it for a second. If you have a customer who needs what you are selling, and one that has absolutely no need for your product. Which one will you convert into a buyer and close faster?

The customer who clearly benefits from the product is ready to part with his money for the solutions that you have offered. Not only both of you are going to be happy at the end. This fast transaction will ultimately increase the amount of customers you service, it will generate you more commission, more confidence in your ability to help people, more enthusiasm in continuing doing your job. You will now see and understand the difference between selling to help versus lying.

This positive attitude will reflect on your confidence. Your new inspired attitude will boost your performance. It is like a self-propelling circle of achievement. The more you do it the right way, the better you get at it and the more you earn. **Commit to loving sales, understand that you are there to help. You are there to make peoples dreams come true!**

Sell to Yourself Your Product First

1.) Even the World's TOP investor is Sold on his Product
2.) Do not let your prospect sell you his situation better than you will sell him your product.

Even the World's TOP investor "is sold" on his Product - Would you believe that the world's most successful investor is young because he drinks at least five Cokes a day? It happens to be that as the media says, the Warren Buffets strange diet is an incredibly smart sales move. He "is being SOLD" on his product first!

From his words, at 84 years old, he wakes up every day and faces the planet with tons of energy: "I'm one quarter Coca-Cola," he says.

This is how his speech begins, and this is an example of how you must engrave in your mind the idea about "being sold" on your product.

The first sale you make, is selling yourself on the benefit of selling. The second sale only, is for your product!

Since we already discussed that, you must believe in yourself as a sales expert and for that, you will believe in your product. I will take the opportunity and explain in this chapter, exactly what you need to be sold on whatever it is you are selling. That, with some mind blowing examples!

Here is another small story to illustrate the point:

It was a Sunday afternoon, and as a salesman, I was working, because that is when everyone has time on his or her hand and comes to the store. It was a regular afternoon, and I was in the business of selling luxury fashion items at that time. I was going through the daily checklist and preparing myself, the store, as a customer came in.

It was a beautiful family, not because the way they were dressed but because everyone was wearing a smile. Therefore, I did the best I could, greeted them with a big smile and welcomed them. Gave them some time to look around and asked the husband how their day was going. To which he silently replied with a chuckle "We are having a great day, but it is probably going to change when my wife and kids decide to buy something".

Oh, and I perfectly knew what he was talking about. Having spent my first 20 years of life in Moldova, were people hardly had money to buy food I knew exactly how he felt. In addition, I supported him, I thought that I will go on now and build a great conversation, and a great relationship and I will make him happy… **Moreover, before I could blink they were already on their way out with even bigger smiles and I had sold nothing to them. I lost the sale…**

As the husband was about to exit the store, he turned around and spoke the words that engraved into my mind: "I am sure glad you did not push us to buy from your store, you probably believed in our happiness more than you did in the things around here, thank you for that.".

It literally blew my mind. **How many other times have I lost a sale until that moment, because I convinced myself of the visitors' situation instead of being sure and convinced about the benefit of my product and how they could use it to their advantage.**

That family did not have to get upset if they bought something, not if I genuinely cared for them and solved their problems. At the end of the day, they entered the store because they had a problem. They wanted to buy some clothes and they wanted to buy the ones that they needed. Since I allowed myself to be convinced, that they did not need my products, they thanked me for genuineness and sincerity and I remained broke.

I decided that they do not need that product, not them. I also passively convinced them that they are better off without it.

Important question you should ask yourself, "**Do you own anything that your company produces?**" Did you buy anything from the company you work? If you did not buy, you do not believe in your products. I know you tell yourself this is the best product out there an all of that and others. However, when the customer comes in and they truly explain to you and give you a thousand reasons like the family in the story above. Somewhere deep, deep in your heart, you will feel for them and they will pick on that immediately. Next thing you will break and you will lose your sale.

Do not let your prospect sell you his situation better than you will sell him your product. - Pay double attention to what you just read. Your prospect will sell you his situation, better than you will sell him your product if you are not prepared.

A buyer is a very good salesman at the same time. Because he sold himself on his experiences, he "is sold" on his condition. He is living the truth of the results of his past actions, buying. He is honest about it because he has real life experience, to which he relates. He saw with his own eyes, heard with his own ears and felt with his own skin. Have you done the same with your product?

You will never be even close to how convinced he is about his situations, unless you buy something your company has produced and experience it for yourself. Trying a product for a short period is not enough unless you buy it. **You have to put yourself in the shoes of the customer when he sacrifices his money to get what you are selling and then see why that money are worth it.**

I cannot stress this enough, to persuade your customer you have to "be sold" on your product, more than he "is sold" on his condition that makes him, say "NO". Because ultimately selling is an exchange of personal beliefs and emotions, and whose beliefs will be stronger, those will prevail.

Believe in your product more than any of your customer believes in their objections and you will close often!

Starting a Conversation with Your Prospect

How do you start a conversation the right way?

A fairly simple and basic question which all companies talk about in their daily, weekly and yearly training no matter what country those are in. What is disappointing the most up until now is how so many companies tell their associates to ask questions that instantly make the customer defensive. First, I will show one example of "a company recommended conversation starter" and then I will discuss it by describing a story related to it.

1.) NOT "The Million Dollar Question"
2.) Questions & Statements - Good Conversation Starters

NOT "The Million Dollar Question" - "How may I help you?"

I cringe when I hear sales associates use it. I love it when they think; adding the word "how" makes it an open-ended question. Try to remember how many times you have had a truly fruitful conversation that started with "How may I help you?" Alternatively, how many times has the customer jumped into describing passionately something they love, need and absolutely must buy. Most probably, your answer is one in a hundred. If you are selling expensive or luxury goods, your answer is "never". Questions like "How may I help you?" just do not cut it these days.

Why does this happen? Why customers do not like you asking them these questions?

Every time a customer starts speaking with the sales executive and is asked the question "How may I help you?" or its derivatives. He or she will answer most of the time "I am just looking."

In such situation, the customer usually gets an average if not lousy experience from the untrained sales associate and then they leave. Next shop, the same thing happens again, then again, and one more time... Until the customer already has a reflex, where their subconscious mind tells them something in these lines:

"Watch out, you are dealing with an untrained sales associate, he just asked you THAT question. Remember what happened last time they asked it?"

So the customer gets defensive. They build up their walls against an interaction and start searching for clues that prove to them, this sales associate is just as bad as the previous sales associate is.

Have a look back. Just because you ask the wrong question everyone else asks, you will get the treatment everyone else gets. A very intuitive result when it comes to human behavior if you ask me.

If you are serious about to becoming the #1 Sales Expert in your field, you cannot be like everyone else. You have to set yourself apart, you have to be better and you have to show this to the customer, by asking different and personalized open-ended questions. You simply ask a question, which nobody else is likely to ask. That is right, simple isn't it?

Example:

I will now illustrate a story where Bob (the sales executive) will perform at his best. If he is lucky, he will close the sale of the day:

A person named Ted walks along the alley of Luxury Retail stores when he finally bumps into the store where Bob was working and decides to enter. As he walks in, the security greets him and sees Bob, the sales associate. Even though Bob was busy, he dropped his work instantly and attended Ted with a big smile. Ted appreciated the importance Bob gave him.

As they walked toward each other, after about 3 to 4 steps, what happened next was magic... What happened next made Ted's day different.

Bob said, "Hello Sir, and welcome. What a great day outside isn't it?" Moreover, off course Ted answers "Yes", it was a good day after all.

So now, Ted is in a positive mood, he said his first "Yes", which makes him more open to saying "Yes" again. Bob just made Ted happy; Bob just loaded the first bullet into his sale gun.

Nevertheless, Bob does not stop there, he continues to be different and build trust with the customer first. Instead of asking him something about his needs, Bob genuinely wants to know how Ted feels. Therefore, he simply goes ahead and says, "I am sure you have had a great day so far, how was it?" Ted just dropped his jaw; people in this store are really giving him full attention and are thinking about his feelings and not about how to sell him the products. At least that is what Ted thinks.

As a sales associate, you are there to attend the customers' needs, and we all have the need to feel good about ourselves.

Bob & Ted start a small conversation of about 3 minutes and they end up speaking about how hot it is outside and how hot Ted feels in his shoes. Bob does not think too much about it. He starts asking question like "What don't you like about those shoes?" and "Which kind of shoes would you prefer to be wearing now?" Without realizing, Ted gives him all the information needed to close the sale. Bob ends up closing the sale by bringing two choices and asking Ted which one he likes more. After Ted chose one, Bob closed him by asking "Should I keep or remove the tags?"

Pay attention. Bob just used this very smart question. It gives Ted 2 options and both of them assume he has already purchased the product. This is what you call a "closing" question. The more you know of these the better it is for you!

Ted bought.

We will have a separate chapter dedicated for closing techniques in this book where you will find a general outline of what these are and how to use them.

Let us review what Bob did in bullet points:

1.) **Bob greeted Ted in a different way, and asked him an open-ended question.**
2.) **Bob asked them customer about himself first. With just another question Bob is not "just another sales associate". Now, he is a conversation partner for Ted.**
3.) **Bob continues to ask questions and uses every opportunity to direct the conversation towards the product, thus not wasting his and his customers' time.**
4.) **Bob makes and offer according to Teds needs and asks for the purchase.**
5.) **Ted purchased.**

The main thing you should understand from this small story is that you have to be genuinely interested about the customers' needs. Not only his material needs but also his needs as a person. Think how you would imagine the best service when you enter a store, and mirror that on your customers. In addition, remember, some customers need you to keep quiet and just give them what they want, more often than you think.

Questions & Statements - Good Conversation Starters

Questions: - Used for more relaxed customers that might have a few minutes for small talk. Such conversation starters are good for outside sales, when you visit the customer or you meet them out of the office.

Examples:

- "How is your day?"
- "Did you have your coffee this morning?" – Use it with returning customers or friendly ones.
- "How are you doing today?" – Use this question with anyone.
- "What kind of watch is that?" – Use this question on customers who are rich and who obviously carry a watch.
- "You look very happy today. How is the weather outside?" – Use this question with anyone, who is not upset.

At the same time, avoid at any cost asking questions about product needs from the beginning. Use statements about your products instead. Instant questions about needs set a boring tone for the conversation and the customer will label you as "Just another sales associate". Show your prospects that you value their time, by giving them the necessary information before they ask for it. See "The Statements" up next.

Statements: - Mostly used for customers who are in a hurry.

NOTE: Most of your customers are in a hurry. These conversation starters are good for indoor sales. When the customer comes to your office/store where all the products are already on display.

Examples:

- "The X products are on this side and the Y products are over there. Let me know if you will need any help."

- "Hello, my name is Andrei. Let me know when you will require assistance."
- "The NEW products are here, and the ones from the last season are there."
- "Let me know when you have decided which of the XYZ you like the most."
- "Let me know when you need more information about what interests you in our store.

There are many more examples that you can derive from these questions and statements. If you need help to start a conversation in a particular environment or case, feel free to contact me on social media channels.

@Andrei_Mungiu – for Twitter

Andrei Mungiu (Author) – For Facebook Page

I will gladly answer all your questions and listen to your valuable feedback.

Don't Speak to Speak - Speak to Sell

Have you experienced a situation when you are speaking to your prospect for a good amount of time, but you cannot establish a deeper connection with them?

The customer was not comfortable to start speaking with you about his needs or his problems. You just had a casual small talk and he or she ended up leaving without buying. If you had these situations, you are not alone. Many of us think that a conversation will always naturally progress into a valuable exchange of information. More than that, most of us tend to think that the conversation will naturally progress in the direction that we need. Big mistake, especially if you are a salesman!

A common belief the average salesman has: "The more you speak, the better you get to know each other and the more likely your customer will buy from you."

That is ONLY true, when you have a daily small talk outside working hours with the same person for many times. This conversation will indeed turn into a long and meaningful chat. However, from personal experience, the same small talk will never turn into a meaningful conversation at work. The chances of small talk to progress towards a sale are zero. I have outlined the reasons next.

When you are at work, there are too many distractions:

1 – You have many "TO do's" pending that keep your brain partly focused on them. You cannot therefore relax and take your time to "chat". Unless you focus specifically on directing the conversation towards the "sale", you are never going to hit it. Your words and thoughts will be like a ship in the storm, going left and right without knowing when it will all end.

2 – The customer does not come to you for a chat, they have a problem to solve and that is the reason why they went out shopping that day or why they accepted you in for a conversation. Assuming they know you is selling XYZ.

Considering both points, you can clearly see how to save your time and your customers time, and even earn their respect for doing your job well. Make you conversation quick, profound and have a direction.

Would you like to know how to have a quick, profound and directed conversation?

WARNING: You should only use this when your customer has time for a chat. If they want to buy straight away, just give them what they want. The faster you do it, the better it is for you and them.

- Greet the customer with a worm and respectful manner. This sets the stage for making them drop down their "salesman shield".
- Start the conversation with an open-ended question or a statement as discussed in the previous chapter. When done correctly, you will be speaking about anything else but your product and for not more than two minutes. How do you know when enough is enough? If you prospect laughed, smiled or suddenly started speaking allot, it means their "salesman shield" is down. It is time for you to pull out your sale gun.
- Your next step would be to switch the conversation towards the sale. For that, you will "probe" the grounds by making a casual comment about your work, what you do, what you sell or what you thought his needs are. It is very important to make this comment using the exact same tone of voice & body language you have used throughout the conversation to this point. Any abrupt or aggressive interruption will ring an alarm in their brain. "Attention, Salesman"

- If your customer does not react, you have to continue dropping these hints more and more often until ignoring them is already impossible.
If they are not willing to buy, you should not waste your time with them. When you value your time, your prospect will have more respect for you in return. They will respect you for not chasing down every bone they throw at you. They will understand that you are there to do business.
If you think that is too aggressive, you had better change your views on sales now. Unless you are that aggressive, when the moment is right, you will never raise above average. Your prospects will label you as a salesman willing to ask for a sale on their knees.
- After you have successfully managed to switch the conversation in the direction of a sale, it is time for you to give them information. Do it!
- Your last step is simple. With a big smile and allot of confidence, ask them if they have all the information they need to make a decision. When they say "Yes", pass the pen and say: "Great, I need you signature here. Let's do this!"

Any small mistake in one of these processes will bring the "salesman shield" up and will make your customer stone cold towards you. With every mistake in this process, your chances for a deep conversation or a final successful close are diminishing dramatically.

The common reason why salesmen fail – The customers will not open up to you, even if you were polite and gave them all the information. **Customers do not need all the information**. Even though it is part of the full process, I kept this point for the end. Most salesmen ignore it and fail at it so hard.

- To correct this mistake, you must ask **drill-down** or **diving** questions. We will call these questions that way because that is what they do. They virtually make you dive deeper into the subject your customer is describing, clarifying any uncertainties or vague statements.

When should you ask a diving question and how?

First, you need to have all your senses connected to the conversation with the customer, no distractions. Every word a customer says should sink into your mind and you must clearly understand its meaning. When you are that attentive and you hear something you do not understand, or even if you understood but you know the answer was very vague, that is when you shoot the diving question.

Example:

Bob is talking to Ted. He managed to get him to open up, converse easily, and share all the details he asked him. Since Bob is smart enough to maintain the conversation, he keeps on asking open-ended questions that push the customer closer to selecting the product, closer to the sale.

Bob: "So tell me what your most important needs are when it comes to purchasing a pair of shoes?"

Ted: "I am mainly looking for comfort and simplicity."

Pay attention as Bob realizes this is the perfect moment to ask a diving question.

Bob: "What exactly do you mean by comfort, which part of the shoe seems to annoy you the most? Or tell me what types did you have previously that you have a lasting positive memory of".

Ted: "Well I have had shoes of brand "X" those where pretty good, the way they picked my size was something different and they nailed it.

Bob: "What exactly was different in the size you purchased at that time, from sizes or models you usually buy?"

… This went on for 5 minutes of back and forth communication between Ted and Bob. At one point, Bob clarified if the demands he got from Ted were correct, and repeated them back to Ted in his own words.

Bob: "Did I understand correctly that you want a shoe that is "XYZ"?

This over here is a VERY powerful technique. When you feed back to the customer what they tell you in your own words, magic will happen. First, you will demonstrate the importance in taking your time to understand them. Second, the customer will say yes. Which means, "Yes, you have understood my needs correctly I trust you with what you are going to bring to the table".

As soon as Bob gets a "Yes", he brings the items he is sure will solve Teds' problem. Than Bob asks for the purchase.

Example:

Bob: "These are exactly what you are looking for; they all meet all your criteria. Which one of them should I pack for you?"

NOTE:

This is the "More options close". When you give the customer more options to choose from assuming he will buy one for sure.

Bob strikes a sale, and creates a satisfied customer who will ask for Bob next time, because Bob talks business.

To recap:

1. Search for vague statements in a customer's answer and ask diving questions, ask for clarification.
2. Feed back to the customer what you just heard in your own words and wait for a confirmation that you understood correctly.
3. Close the sale.

Go out and see how this magic works, let me know on social media how this chapter helped you!

How to Redirect a Drifting Conversation Back to Closing

In other words, do not fail to sell.

Let us start by looking at a short story where Bob the salesman did everything correctly, but something about his conversation was not leading him in the correct direction. Let us see how Bob tries to learn and understand what is happening as he goes. After all, he did not yet read as much about sales as you will now.

As one day Ted, the prospect, comes back to the shop, Bob happens to be at work and greets him warmly. Everything is great, the conversation flows naturally and Bob is carefully implementing his diving questions again.

Bob perfectly advances the conversation as Ted keeps on relating to him about his world travels and describes some of the countries he visited in depth. Ted is describing those moments not because he wanted, but specifically because Bob asked diving question about those subjects.

After nearly two hours, of what Bob thought was a fruitful conversation:

Ted. "Bob, it was a pleasure talking to you; I can only hope to meet you again and have one more conversation as we had today.

Both said their good byes and parted shaking hands.

Bob FAILED to sell!

Why did Bob fail?

Bob just spent 2 hours of his working time, which is exactly 25% of his workday on a conversation that did not bring him any money. Sure, you might say that since that was a returning customer having a conversation with him without pushing him to purchase is something any respectful person would do. That is wrong and exactly the opposite of what you must do if you want to make money at work instead of making broke friends.

Alternatively, imagine that Bob was so good at establishing customer relationships, that after two years in the industry he had more than 200 friends who casually dropped by. Not only is Bob bound to lose at least 25% of his time on a daily basis, because he "trained" his customer to chat long hours with him. Now the customers expect this every time they visit the shop.

Consequently, Bob created around himself a circle of people that want to chat more than they want to buy.

The moment Bob will want to change that or will try to cut the conversation short, no matter how polite or how advanced techniques he will use. Customers like Ted will feel upset. Not only will Bob lose all his time investments he made so far, his investments were in the wrong direction all along. Those entire negative results surfaced, because Bob did not direct the conversation the right way.

What should Bob do to WIN in SALES?

What he should have done is discipline himself to spend a maximum of 10% of the time on building a friendly conversation and the rest on persuading the customer to buy. In addition, as the conversation progressed he should have asked question that would inevitably make the customer speak about his product needs.

Example:

As Bob speaks to Ted about what countries he visited, Bob realizes he must move closer to making the sale so he asks, "I see you really had the time of your life. Tell me Ted, how were the shoes you bought from us last time, in your travels? Are you happy with the quality?" – The subject of Teds' product is now open.

To master this, you must practice again, and again, and again! Therefore, I have prepared a simple exercise up next that will change how you view sales at 180 degrees!

Practice exercise:

Think about situations and conversation where your conversation drifted and you ended up speaking too much and sold too little. Play those situations in your mind as detailed as you can, specifically try to remember the exact dialogue. As you think about it, look for moments where you could ask a redirecting question like the one shown in the previous example.

The question will connect the subject your customer was speaking about with the product you were trying to sell. Write that question down on paper and think about the differences. The moment you do that, I guarantee you will truly feel like a real sales expert. No longer will sales be haphazard activity for you. A sale is a science and it requires you to study it, if you want to achieve an expert level.

Can you now understand why time equals money? Good! Start Selling!

Closing Explained

This is the decisive moment! You have prepared so far for this moment.

The last step of any sales conversations is the close. In other words, making them give you the cash or swipe the card. Oh yes... that great feeling when you know that you are about to get it. There is only one-step left for you to take. However, you do not know which one it is do you?

You can see the customer biting their lips or holding the product in their hands and you can almost hear two sides of their mind battling between purchasing it or not. So what is it that you must do now?

Listen to this carefully! Persuading happens when you speak, buying happens when you ask the right question!

Examples:

- "Would you like to have that delivered now or should we delay... and have it shipped after a month?"

- "Would you like someone to deliver your car home or, would you like to drive home in this new Cadillac now?"

Buying happens when you ask the right question!

It is not only about what you ask, it is how you ask it and when you ask it. **The question should remove any obstacle a buyer might have, it should always give them a choice between two, of which both will make him buy.**

As you have seen in the last two examples, they have the options of choosing what service they require and both options will prove positive towards your sale.

When do you push for closing?

Hey, so when should you push for the close?

Avoid closing too early; and avoid closing too late.

Closing too early happens when you have not invested the minimum 10% of communication to establish rapport with the customer. By asking diving questions not related to the product of their interest. Last but and not least, before the moment of closing you should have asked a sufficient amount of questions to perfectly understand the customers' needs and offer them exactly what they want, the price being the least of concerns. Moreover, even though many sales executives do that, they lose the sale because they are afraid to close and they end up closing too late or not closing at all.

When you have the customer trusting you, when you have the product they need before their eyes, you also need to have the guts to push them to it. Give them a little notch in the right direction. Sometimes that notch will mean you have to remove the discomfort of making them choose. **Therefore, you will simply act as if they already made their choice and ask how they would like it delivered.**

On the other hand, if they cannot decide between two or more, bring out all the confidence you can muster and with a deep down voice tell that you genuinely think they should go for A because you had Ted who made the same choice and now walks around happing owning what you recommended.

Whatever the obstacle in the final decision is, apply this only for the final decision.

You must act as if obstacles are not there or the solution to them is very simple. The way you perceive the difficulty of closing a sale, the same way the customers feels about deciding to buy.

Do you ask why?

If you cannot decide yourself as the expert, it means there is something wrong or you are not sure of it. When the expert is not sure, nobody will give money for what even the expert does not have confidence in it.

The Owner Close, involves you making the customer picture how they will feel already owning the product or service, and using its benefits. If they can do that, your chances of winning the deal have just double in a blink.

You must understand that closing in not necessarily just the last sentence that you use to strike the sale. Closing could be several attempts that lead you to the result. It is also not about using a specific technique as the owner close. The close is about genuinely pushing the customer with all your force and knowledge to purchase what you have offered. Because you know, that after all the effort you put into understanding their needs, you have offered exactly what will solve their problems. If they do not take it now, not only will you not sell, you will miss the opportunity of giving them a happier life. You will miss the opportunity to set them free of their problems and they will walk away never knowing what they missed. **You are there to make sure your customer understands all of that so well, that deciding to buy is not a doubt but a necessity to make their life easier.**

Be confident, to the extent of being irrationally about it if you must! Do not let the buyer sell you their inability to buy instead of you selling them the perfect solution.

Selling to People who do not Speak Your Language

One important skill every master salesperson has to have, is selling to those who do not speak his native language.

Not everyone you encounter these days can fluently speak your language. With the current internationalization and drive to reduce traveling times and costs, the biggest challenge would be to know how to sell, know how to push your product correctly, to those who cannot speak your language.

Throughout my experience as a sales expert, in countries where only 2% to 5% of people are local population, I have understood the following: **The simpler you can describe your product, the more likely they are to buy it.**

If a person is even average, at understanding the language you speak, your best bet is to keep it short and keep it simple.

You will not keep aside all your selling techniques. On the contrary, this is the time where you have to apply all of them, but from a different perspective. You do not speak a language anymore; in fact, you should not speak in any other language as much as you speak the body language. **This means minimal verbal implications**.

Example:

If I was currently selling a product to an Arabic customer who happens to know just the basics of English, I will greet them and make sure to present myself, as a well-mannered person. **MANNERS = BODY LANGUAGE**. This does not require a speech at all, if only a few words.

When they go to the product and ask about it, my comments will be short and straight to the point. I will avoid telling stories that might confuse and consequently make them unsure of buying. **Most likely, I will push for the close without building any rapport,** because they will not understand me.

Whenever I will speak, it will confuse and have them wander if everything is ok with the product. Alternatively, maybe I am trying to point out something that they might not like. You never know if what they understood is what you said. Keep it simple and straight to the point.

I remember noticing, how one of the customers started looking at me with a puzzled look. In that moment, I thought about all the communication skills I was using, and how I was **overusing** them. Therefore, I made it a point that day to keep it simple and keep it short. I greeted the next customer with a big smile and not a single word. When asked if the product was suitable for their needs I shortly and enthusiastically said, "This is the best choice you could have ever made; can I either wrap it as a gift now or just keep it in a bag for you."

Do you know what she replied?

"Just put it in a bag, and let me pay for it quick."

Do not try to overflow the customer with information; always check if they already made a decision. You do not need to make your "Full product presentation" or throw at them all the "Product knowledge you have" before they can decide.

I decided what car to buy over the internet without even setting one foot in any auto show. Imagine if the sales executive there will start speaking too much and spoil all my enthusiasm of getting in the car and driving away. You know what will happen. I will just ask another person to assist in closing the deal faster.

Everyone these days wants things and problems handled fast. **If you are not fast, you will be last!**

Back to the example, it was the fastest sale that I have made in that week. Then I did it a second time and third time and fourth, so I suddenly started seeing this pattern. People who could not communicate my language appreciated allot if my feedback was short and to the point. **All I had to do is encourage them to follow their first choice and without even explaining say that I also think, it is a good choice that they have made.**

Ever since that day, I understood the one and most important thing: **Not everyone wants your "Customer relationship"; most people just want to buy and go enjoy it!**

The True Story Behind Price

Price objections do not exist. The objection is never about price.

Just because the customer is complaining, does not mean they will not buy it. I complain about expensive products all of the time, you do as well. Nevertheless, we all buy what fulfills our needs not just what is cheaper. A fair point of view, do you think?

When there is a "Sale", the amount of customers flowing in suddenly rises. So many products sell, and everyone is so busy. However, the profit margin, the pure profit after is only a little higher. Compare this to the exerted effort on selling the products; you get much less money for much more work.

A "Sale" after all, is more of a "Plan B" for the company. Therefore, it does not make a loss by throwing away unsold products. The fat profit, comes when the customer is convinced to pay the full price and even more. Do not drop price, increase offer quality!

To make life easier, I have categorized all buyers in two camps, **discount buyers and loyal buyers**.

Your **loyal buyers are those who come to you because of the customer relationship that you have built with them**. They come to you, because of the love for the product and service that you are offering. A loyal buyer is a repeated customer who cares more for quality of product, quality of service and reputation. These represent about 95% of the people.

Off course, the loyal buyer get even more quantity when the prices are lower. However, the total amount of money they spend will be almost the same. Many of the loyal buyers would buy the exact same amount in value, even if the prices were higher.

Selling discounted items, technically only damages their profit margin. Profit margin being the amount of money you have on hand, after you covered all the costs of doing business.

This leaves for the second camp of buyers, **the 5% of buyers who are price hunters. These people are rarely concerned with the real quality of items.** As long as the item is in good shape, they are not interested in the story behind the product or your customer service. These people want the transaction done fast, so they can get back to their business of jumping from flower to flower, buying products with the lowest price. Trying to convert the price hunter into a loyal customer will most of the time prove lucrative and not worth the effort.

If the price hunter converts himself, that is good. However, it is rarely worthy of going the extra mile in trying to win them over. You will end up dropping your price lower than you can, ultimately hurting your brand image and your budget.

So what do you do when a loyal customer comes in and complains about the price? You have two choices.

1. **Handle the price objection as a complaint.** Hear what the customer has to say and continue moving towards the Point Of Sale while doing it.

When your prospect is saying, "The price is too high". You have to understand: That is only a comment they are making about the product. Their decision to want this product has not changed. Therefore, you do what a professional salesperson in this case would. You continue your closing by inviting them to finalize the transaction now.

Observe in that moment, how easy it is for a customer to go along and buy. You have convinced them the product is worth the initial price. Make no mistake; your customer still remembers that the price is high, so why do they buy it anyway? They buy because they want it and because they like it. **People do not buy based on logic, they buy based on emotions.**

2. **Weed out the real objection, and point it out to the customer.** Help them understand, what they are really looking for is not price, but a reason to pay the current price.

Example:

"Mr. Prospect, setting the price aside, do you feel satisfied with the overall quality and utility of the product? Does it fulfill all your needs?"

Most of the time, the customer will say "No". Perfect, go ahead and ask the real reason why they are not buying that product. What you are about to do is very important, if you do not, you will lose the magic moment and the sale. You have to identify what they want, and give them a product that will fulfill all their needs, no matter if the price of that new product is higher!

When you present this new product, do not even mention the price. Simply say that it will meet all their needs and ask them how they would like it delivered.

If however, their answer to your question from above is "Yes". Meaning the initial product does fulfill all their needs. Ask them what feature they would give up from the product if you were to offer them something at a lower price.

Another magical moment will happen; the prospect will be against you dropping any features. At that point, explain; if they really want the product that fulfills all their needs, it will only cost a small premium for full satisfaction.

Example:

"Ms. X, the difference between product A and B is 100$, and for only 100$ more your get all your needs satisfied, for 100$ less you spend 900$ in vain. It would be a good idea to buy 900$ with 100$, what do you think?

In other words, they both buy at the original price and are satisfied, or they pay less and lose all their money. Put your customer in that situation while passing along the pen and paper saying, "Sign over here". Customer closed – happy end!

Example #2:

"Mr. or Ms. X, I believe that it is in your interest to spend the right amount of money, and get exactly what you are looking for. Than spend a little bit less and lose all the benefits of being fully satisfied."

Again, a customer is always looking to fulfill their needs. The price can never be too high; it is the product, which might not be worth such price. As a sales expert, find the product that makes your prospect happy, stop looking for lower prices.

I remember visiting my former colleague as he was in the middle of a sales conversation. The man was looking to buy a suit. My friend, the sales associate, was desperately trying to present him all the features and benefits, of every suit, one by one. In a particular moment, the customer decided all prices were too high. Than the sales associate grabbed a cheaper suit and explained, how that one should fit his budget. The prospect looked away.

If I would not interfere in that moment, he would have lost the sale. I approached the person and greeted him, presented myself as a fan of suits and told him all about the collection of suits I had at home. I explained, what he should really do is try another suit, giving him the most comfortable fit I knew they had in store for him.

I never said a word about the price. He looked in the mirror and observed how this one fitted his body superbly. Having the same body as him, I explained how I was constantly using that specific cut to have a more elegant and stylish look. We ended up speaking about how amazing all the small detail were and how you could see the enormous amount of work done by the tailor in every inch of stitching.

He went to the counter, when the teller mentioned the price he did not even look sideways or stop, he simply payed for what he thought was fulfilling all his needs.

So how exactly was my friend about to lose that sale?

He viewed himself as someone who is there to find "a good deal" for the customer instead of giving them the "best deal". A salesman will think about selling the product which inevitable drives him to offer cheaper and cheaper prices In the hope that a smaller price will convince the customer to buy, now that works some of the times but most of the times it does not, specially not after you have shown them something better. I have viewed myself on the contrary and a problem solver, I knew the man's problem was getting a suit to represent him well, so I offered him what he was looking for. He later explained how happy he was that he finally found something that met all his needs, and said nothing about searching for a cheap product.

A few good conclusions from this article:

Give your customer all the alternative products and not all the alternative prices. You want to use up your entire inventory in the process of giving him what he needs because the moment he find exactly what will solve his problem he will pay more than what you think that product is worth.

Ever heard about people complaining how they went out to buy something and they did not buy anything at the end of the day, not because the prices were too high but because they did not find what they were looking for? I heard that many times and I have personally experienced it as well. Keep that in mind the next time someone tell you the price is too high.

People will buy when the value that they think the product is worth is higher than the price you ask for it. Quite simply if you offer someone an ice cream that costs 10$ and he thinks it is not worth more than one$ at that moment he will not buy it in 10 lifetimes. The same ice-cream that costs 10$ could be worth a 100$ to him if he knew that he just had to get one or he will have to bare the heat of the sun without refreshments for another 2 hours.

The price for the product should be as high as it is acceptable for the customer, taking into account the purchasing power of the individual and the external factors.

Second Money - Easier Than First Money

Many sales experts ignore this subject and only few sales seminars mention it. Yet it is the most important point you need to know after you have successfully mastered the art of closing a transaction.

The reason second money is so easy, is because the customer has already opened up to spending and is in the positive mood to do it again. Make someone say "yes" several times before you get a "yes" to your most important question. Well the same is valid regarding sales. When people spend money, they feel good. In addition, the better they feel the more like they are to spend again!

This is why, one of the main KPI in organizations is the variable called Units per Transaction. It simply measures the amount of units a customer had bought at one time. In different industries, this number will change. However, no matter what the price is, the fact is that the second purchase is always easier than the first one. I am telling you this from my personal experience and you are about to understand how exactly I came across it.

Remember one of those big transactions when someone bought a huge amount of unit's vs someone who bought just one unit. The amount of effort you wasted on both of them is most likely equal. That is because you will put the biggest into setting the buyer into a buying state! After you do that, it is all about closing them the right way and pushing the right buttons to make them buy what you have to offer.

The process of working with any customer is like opening up a chest. You need to find the key called trust, before you can open the chest called cash.

Think about the customer as a chest; once you open it up, you have access to everything that is inside as resources, benefits, and knowledge. You can start a conversation with them virtually about anything. Then work on uncovering some other subconscious needs for products, which you might be able to satisfy. At the very least, you have to understand that it is your duty to offer them a complimentary product, not for the sake of selling but for the sake of their own good. When you have put all this effort, to show that what you have offered is good. This means that you are on the right track to making their life easier to making them happier. So why not double your impact and offer them even more solutions?

This is exactly the point where a professional sales man differs from an amateur. An amateur allowed society to brain wash him that selling is detrimental, that it is a sneaky way of stealing. Moreover, even if publicly the amateur might look proud about his profession deep down inside he has a small voice that tells him: "You are lying to the customer, you are making a fraud, and you are stealing away money from them." This is absolute bull.

Resolve right now; that you will refuse to become that kind of a sales man. Refuse to have such lack of product knowledge that you are unsure of what you are doing when you are selling. It must be clear to you, clear as the waters in a mountain lake, that what you are doing is exactly what the customer wants. For that, you must know your product well. Know all of its features and benefits. Not for telling your customer, a 2 hour story about it, but for knowing yourself with confidence that your customer is going to have all those benefits.

Customers are rarely paying for something that only "looks" good. They want the product to be worth much more than they pay for it. They want to believe in all the efforts that someone put into creating a solution for them. Materials from around the world had to be gathered, workforce from different countries had to work, the logistics of the greatest companies came together to deliver this product to your customer. They are not just buying a product; they are buying everything else that goes with it!

If you will know what the customer wants, and you will apply your communication skills perfectly, ask questions and make them open up for their own good. You will eventually offer your prospect what they really need, not just what they want.

When you are able to confidently and with clear truth in your heart, say that you have done all your best to offer a solution for your customer, and you have explained to them in all the ways why it is so important and crucial for them to have their problems solved with that product. You will not just make sale, you will truly fulfill the call of a professional sales man.

At such moment in time, you can sell to your customer as many solutions as you can. By following the same process, with truth in your heart and total conviction that you are doing the right thing, you will sell. **Second money is the easiest money indeed, only if you can prove to your customer that you act from the best of your intent.**

Second money is almost as guaranteed money! All you have to do is decide that you are not asking them to spend more; you are asking them to have one more problem solved instead of letting them go home with problems on their back. Solve your customers problems at once, be genuine about letting your customer go with all their problems solved and they will rain money on you.

Time, Health & Sales

What is the energy that drives expert salesman? What is the reason they are performing so well?

I am glad you have asked that question, we are going to discuss and analyze it now.

First, let us define that the blood of anything you do is a resource. During my researches of what exactly a resource in a sales executive's life would be, I have found that the resources we as a sales experts have and use on a daily basis are three.

These are:

- **Time**
- **Health**
- **Money**

Any activity that you do at work, in fact any activity that you are involved in throughout the day will use all of these three. Now the first thing I want you to understand is that all of these are limited. This means there is a certain limit of them you have on a daily basis. To generate any results you will use more or less from one or the other. By the time, your daily limit is finished. Example, either you go to sleep because there is no time or you are exhausted, or you have no money to continue what you are doing you will have generated some results.

Time – the time you have is limited. The day you were born the clock started ticking and the time you have will continuously run away from you. Like a sand watch that slowly but confidently loses send from the top going to the bottom. Every choice that you make on a daily basis will affect this resource. If you think of it now, it is impossible to make a decision that would not delete time. You choose to sell, manage, read a book, go out for sport or even stay and do nothing. Those all are choices that consume your most invaluable resource, time.

Example:

Life gives us a certain amount of it at birth. Yet by the end of this resource, looking at what an individual has accomplished throughout his life you can understand that most of us put a very small value on their time. The good news is, you do not need to wait until the end of your life to be able to analyze how time was used. You are lucky enough to have an analytical mind that can tell you. If you do nothing, your time is lost. If you get busy, at least your time is not lost, and if you become a professional, your time was used to its maximum. I wrote this book to ensure that you will use your resources properly.

Health – Health is the most sneaky and hidden resource of all. Understanding what exactly influences it is a lifelong study on which you must embark. You may think to yourself, "How is health used when I decide to sell to a customer?"

When you communicate, manage, delegate or perform any task, no matter how small. You are using your mind, your body and your spirit. In addition, we all know what happens when you overuse something as time goes by. A little bit here, a little bit there and by the end of the day, you are tired. You have used your body, your mind, health and now you need some sleep to regenerate. Health as a resource not only depletes when you decide to which task you are going to allocate it. This is why it is such a difficult resource to manage. Health is directly proportional to what you eat, what you drink, how much you sleep, weather you are smoking or not, God forbid, weather you do drugs or not, last but not least weather you consistently practice sports' not. Health in fact, it is the only resource that can positively influence time. That is right, imagine, by taking care of your health you will increase the time you have on your hand.

That is a way to cheat and gain some little bit of immortality. Can you imagine that you can extend the amount of time you have on this planet. You had better start taking care of your health today and to the end of time.

Money – ah, the sound of it makes any salesman vibrate. The more of the other two resources you have as Time & Health, the more of this resource, Money, you can generate. Money is a complex byproduct of your performance; in fact, money is a partial and temporary measure of your performance on how you have been doing to this moment. Look in your bank account now or your wallet. You do not like what you see? That is because so far you have not been administering sufficiently well Time, Health and Money. Lucky you, money are a byproduct and a resource at the same time. You can both control how much you have of it, and the way you administer it. More than that, a successful administration of money would mean investing a good part of it back into developing yourself. For example purchasing this book was one of the best investment you have probably made in terms of developing yourself as a Retail Sales Expert. Money is a resource that can also influence your health, so at this point you can see that all of them are connected. If you fail to administer wrongly at least one of them, the other two will inevitably drop down. However, if you become a master at it, if you understand how to work with all three, you will truly become not only a sales expert but also a master of any craft. Getting a promotion for you will just be a question of time, of very short time in particular.

The results that you have generated are a reflection of how you managed your resources. Decide wisely, at stake is Time, your Health and your Money.

Customer First

Customer satisfaction should be on top of ANYTHING.

When a customer walks in the store, you drop whatever you have been doing so far and focus on them. It does not matter if you were working on preparing the stock for the inventory, or you were having a meeting with the whole team on the shop floor, someone must attend the customer.

Imagine the following story: Bob, who has gone through this book and now perfectly knows how to prepare himself, the environment and everything that will increase his chances of making a sale, decides to continue arranging the stock when a customer just walked in. Effectively, Bob just tossed away everything he learned into the bin. Bob will not implement anything of what he learned.

Off course, Bob could have gone the other way. The moment he saw the customer walk in, he could have dropped what he was doing and acknowledged the customers visit. Only by this, Bob clearly sent a message:

"You are important to me; there is nothing more important than you and your satisfaction in this store".

The customer feels valued and Bob just loaded his first bullet into his sale gun. Next, bob continues to service the customer and he ends up closing the biggest transaction of the year, or did he loose it? That is a decision Bob makes when he is choosing between ignoring the customer, and attending to his needs.

All the effort in the preparation for and during a sale is about directing it at one moment only, the moment when the customer swipes his credit card or hands you in the cash. If that last bit does not happen, no matter what skills you have, no matter how successful the shop placement or the management of the company is, if that does not occur the whole process was pointless, because it did not generate any money.

In sales, it is all about selling, that is why you observe that the head of the company only thinks about sales. And I can understand you, sometimes those guys up there will never think about the sales executive and only scream "Where is my money?", if that is the case, as I talked in the chapters before, ask yourself if you are in the right company. However, no matter how many companies you will change, at the end of the day you are there to make the customer exchange his money for solving his problems.

Therefore, what does it actually mean "customers first"?

You keep hearing about it every day, everyone keeps on telling you about it. Nevertheless, when the time for someone to do it comes few of us actually do it. Well, that is because you have only heard about it and acknowledged that it is a good and logical course of action. However, if you want to arouse your desire to do it, you have to go deeper than that. So Let us break down into several steps.

Why "customer first" is such a crucial thing:

Customer brings money – as I said before, the customer is the one who brings in the money to the organization, your boss does not have money falling on his lap out of the blue sky, and it comes from the company. So understand that by not servicing your customers properly, by not putting their needs first you indirectly throw your salary out of the importance zone. By not servicing your customer, you indirectly are telling everyone around you the following:

"Hey, my salary is not important, I do not care if I get less money or less commission, I already have more than I need."

If you do not have more than you need, than do what you have to do. Put your money first by putting your customers' needs first.

Customer is a resource - The second reason why "customer is first": he is part of the company resources that you have. Your customer is your only way for you to practice the skills you have learned in this book and your only chance to achieve great results. So again, by putting the customer aside, you are throwing away your skills, your experience and you chances of succeeding in this life as a sales expert. If your career is important to you, if you would like to improve your skills, find a better job or pursue the dream of becoming the best salesman in the industry. Do the obvious, put the customer first and watch your life turn around.

Customers need your help – as crazy as it may sound, just as a doctor at his job. You have responsibilities that come along with yours, the salesman job. As a sales executive, you are there to help your customer when they need your help. Just as a doctor gave an oath of saving his dying patients no matter what, the same way the customer relies on your knowledge to solve their problems.

If by any means you do not enjoy solving the problems your customers face at the job you currently work, change the company. Go somewhere, where you are going to enjoy. We have talked about this many times in the book; you will only be able to succeed to the extent that you are enthusiastic and charismatic during your work. Enthusiasm has to be genuine; it has to come sincerely. Find what is so special about your product and how it can change and benefit your customers' lives. Than every time they come in, understand that they are looking for that solution and they desperately need your help. Oh by the way, they are going to pay you good money for that!

Service, service, service and over service your customers. You need to throw at them so much service that they drown in it. Backing up and being shy will not work here, what you need to do is bring your customer a glass of water, ice and paper towel when all he asks for is water. Do not ask the customer if he wants something that will be beneficial for him and you can provide it free, provide it instantly, and provide it before they ask for it.

Add value to your conversation as much as you can by being the most open and helpful person out there. People pay when they perceive the value they get more than the price they pay.

Think about the restaurant you went to with a girlfriend. You wanted to impress here you wanted to win here over. Therefore, if you want here to buy into it, you take here to the best one. You take here were the same food is well served, where the waiter is smiling, were people remember what you have ordered and that they have to deliver it soon. You take here were people don't bother you every 5 minutes asking if you want something more, but stay somewhere far away and the moment you start looking for them they are right in front of you.

You want your customer to buy in as well. Many times, you want them to spend the savings of a lifetime. This especially valid for real estate agents and care salesman from time to time. Their customers want a trust worthy person, a person who is sharp, enthusiastic and knowledgeable.

Moreover, what do the same salesmen do? They cannot dedicate their full and unconditional attention to this customer for at least 20 minutes. Their phone distracts them; they look at the notifications or make a quick look at the recent email they received. Man, you cannot ever hope to succeed if you will not show your customer that he is the center of your universe. Forget about it!

Do not let anything distract you, look at how your customer will acknowledge your efforts and pay you with the same attention back. Learn and train yourself to give 100% attention to the person you are selling something to, avoid chasing two rabbits and politely ignore anyone that wants to interrupt your interaction.

You cannot advertise your way to selling, you need service.

You need service and purpose.

The Confession of a Salesman – Believe in Yourself

First things first, I love being a salesman. Second, was not always like that. Read on if you want to get to where I am!

I remember the day I had to make my first sale as if it was yesterday. A customer was approaching me. I was behind the counter, so scared looking around for someone to come and help. With the luck I had, everyone was busy and unseen; I mean the entire shop was empty. When I looked for help, which I literally did, nobody answered. I felt like I was going to go down through meters of concrete from the embarrassment and fear I had.

The customer brought the merchandise to the table, and asked me to scan them. I started sweating as if I was playing a rugby match. With some unbelievable force and courage, which I thought it was at that time, I managed to bring out a few words from the tip of my throat: "Sir, I don't know what to do.", it sounded worse that an old & rusty door closing slowly during the night... at my grand-grand-grandparents' house. If such a door still exists that is.

After a pause of about five seconds, seeing how the man was looking around for someone else that "wasn't useless", without any consciousness of what I was doing, I added "But those jeans sure look nice, those are my favorite ones, I bought one pair for myself. They are the most comfortable ones I ever had". That very moment, the entire weight dropped from my shoulders.

Nothing can encourage you more to believe in yourself then having truth itself behind your actions.

What followed was a total embarrassment: "I guess you just started with these guys." Said the man, as he took the scanner and did the entire sale by himself. A million thoughts went through my brain at that time; including how worthless of an employee I must have been if even the customers knew more than I did.

I knew that I had to learn something from it, and I did. I realized as a sales noob that trying your product is an absolute must, if confidence and belief in yourself is what you seek in sales.

The jeans were worth it, and **I was sure** he had to get them. As we spoke about it, my speech was clear and eloquent; I was authentic and knew very well that I was telling the truth. There was no reason to be afraid of saying something wrong.

To believe in yourself, you have to persuade your mind about it. Do that by selling the product to yourself first.

How do you do it?

Learn what you are selling well, learn your sales techniques well, but more than that try your product and be genuine about the feedback. Under no circumstances am I saying that if you think your product is bad you should leave it at that. What you should do is sell yourself, on your product, as you would sell a customer. Find the benefits of your product think of how it could benefit your prospect and build your presentation that. Make sure you do not forget to ask the customer what he thinks about it. The last thing you want is sell blue jeans, when all they need is black ones. There are salesmen who do not know that, and I was one of them when I began.

When you finished convincing yourself that, you absolutely love what you are selling. The next step would be to convince yourself that you are, already the most capable man in the world to solve anybody's problems.

You have to be genuinely interested in what a customer's problems are. When you do that, you will automatically start asking them allot of questions, because you care, because you need to know in order to help. Be genuine about helping people that enter your store and they will reward you with their trust and their money.

You have to believe in yourself, with your whole heart and breath. Believe that you are there to help, you are there to solve their problems and only you as an expert in the entire world can do it right there for them. You have to DECIDE that you will not settle for "just enough" when it comes to presenting and convincing. You will not settle for "good", you are here to do everything they need and ten times above.

Have them absolutely convinced that the product is worth even more than the price tag. The moment you do that, they will take it from you with pride. You just convinced them that they stole it from you, that they won the lottery.

People want to feel good, and they will pay more for an amazing experience. An amazing attitude is worth more than an amazing product, it will surely pump your sales to the next level!

Surround yourself with people that believe in you. Surround yourself with events that will allow you to boost your skills and show off your talents, surround yourself with activities that increase your value and allow everyone else to see what good of a performer you are.

What you do should conquer you.

Just as I am writing this book, let your mind freely express your true potential, your experiences.

The #1 reason you do not believe in yourself is that you are afraid, you are afraid that you might make a mistake you are afraid that people might laugh at you. You are not prepared to make a mistake. You think that if something goes wrong your entire life will be miserable.

Then a day comes that you make that mistake, and you feel miserable. Alternatively, maybe you are crying as everyone else is laughing at you. Nevertheless, eventually you will overcome that emotion; you will replace it with new enthusiasm. And just when that new enthusiasm is about to launch you into your greatest achievement in a lifetime, your mind reminds you again about past experiences, your negative thoughts are all over your brain again and off course you fail again. I just paint the exact picture of what being a beginner feels like. Well take good note of it, attitude will make or kill your goals and your dreams. Believe in yourself, and other will believe in you!

Example:

You came home from outside after a good match of football. Back when it was sunny, fun and you were very young, you even forgot about being hungry or thirsty. Well eventually, you get home, you enter the house, and you start eating. As you eat and enjoy your food, suddenly someone, asks you to pass him or her along the ketchup. Moreover, you say, "There is no ketchup" and they say, "Go get it". In addition, you say, "I don't know where it is" – "It is in the kitchen," they say. Therefore, you go into the kitchen, while your mind keeps repeating, "I don't know where this ketchup is I have no idea where this ketchup is.

"It is not here" you shout after a while, they tell you "look in the drawers" you look you can't find it and you "yell" it is not here. Than you father comes, opens the same drawer picks it up right from the front of your nose and asks you "What is this? Huh?" Have you ever had one of those moments? I am sure you did.

So what happened here?

When you repeat a thousand time, you cannot. No it did not, because you have conditioned it that way by repeating many time what it cannot do.

Exactly the same thing happens when you are enthusiastic about something, and then you start being afraid remembering past failures.

Understand, failure is inevitable, failure is a constant, and this is how humans learn their craft. Failure is the constant that show you are trying new things. However, failure is not a result… as long as you keep coming back! Believe in yourself!

I remember hearing some kind of CEO talk with his colleague in the elevator about how he thought the person was not working properly because he did not have a good amount of failures. He did not like that all his projects where successfully, in-fact he told him that it is considered a normal in their organization that for most of the projects to fail. That was a high caliber 40+ years man speaking to his colleague. Believe in Yourself!

Failure is not an option,

Failure is not an option; failure is the road you must overcome to achieve success. There is no shortcut to success through a safe road. If you want to be at the TOP just must have something unique about you. Moreover, you can never become unique if all you will do is walk on paths that others have laid down before you.

Believe in yourself, explore new opportunities, new horizons, you need to gain the experiences that maybe no one else has. You need to make your life a quest to challenging what others have not. Only that way can you discover new things and only that way will you be able to achieve your greatest potential. So get it out of your head, that failure is something negative. Failure is the most valuable form of feedback, which tells you that what you have done did not work and you have to change your game. Change your strategy if you want to places you could not reach so far. Believe in yourself!

Can never find out what the right way is unless you start walking and falling down, just like when England invaded Germany on D-day, countless soldiers have failed and died to construct a road through minefields.

Sure, some of them got lucky, but if none of them would have failed the Second World War might have ended much, much later. Believe in yourself, it takes failure to succeed.

Believe in yourself, believe that you can get up every time you fall down, believe the no matter how hard it might be now the more you fail the close you are do achieving your goal.

Never giving up is the ultimate commitment to believing in yourself, the ultimate key to becoming a master salesman!

Predict

Predicting a situation is what any professional can do. The ability to predict comes from being familiar with your strengths and weaknesses.

So what are the strengths and weaknesses of a salesman?

Gladly, in sales it will be much easier for you to acquire these skills. The customer comes into your territory, which is your training ground, you know every inch of it, and he does not.

Like in war, knowing the battlefield will give you confidence. Which is a massive advantage in closing a sale and convincing someone about the features and benefits of your product.

The first step of understanding the "battlefield" is to recall the interaction that happened. Obviously you cannot always video record, what you can & must do is get a voice recorder! Now I am not advising you to do this IF it is illegal to record someone in your country without his or her knowledge and approval, I advise you to always follow the law. Here I will present you all possible tools that you can use to record your sales conversation, how analyze your recordings and apply your findings in practice the next time you are out for work.

Find a ways to record and recall your sales conversation. The best thing off course would be to videotape and register voices. If videotaping is not possible, a voice recorder will do the necessary quiet well. If for whatever reason you do not want to or cannot use both, you have to use the good old memory and take notes after the interaction.

What are the most important things you need to pay attention too?

1. **Objections** - Every sales conversation will inevitably involve your customer making objections. These can range from expression of reluctance to the products quality, saying they are only looking today, or they do not want to buy in a rush or the world famous, the price is too high. Depending on what products you are selling, you will tailor this objection specifically to your case. The moment you will start recording these interactions, taking notes of the objection you encounter on a daily basis you will start seeing that they are much fewer that you thought. The same objections will come up in a different manner, but they will all carry the same few messages.

Critical point:

Most of the salesmen fail at this point and I was guilty of it in the beginning of my career countless times. After recording, you quickly feel empowered that you "know" what will happen next time. Just because they heard it once, does not mean the next time you will hear it, you will know exactly what to answer... Without taking the slightest effort into actually preparing yourself, you will never become a PRO. How can you expect to have results if you do not have a plan?

What you need to do is take every objection, write it on the paper and then find several possible ways in which you could answer it.

You might think, "I like to keep the conversation flow naturally, I have a "smell" for it and I know what I do. Well I personally never heard about any salesman who would go into an important sales conversation without a plan of what he was going to talk about and walk out of it 100% happy knowing he did his best. Just because he did not prepare he could not do his best by default. You need to have all the answers you those objection written and memorize by heart.

Moreover, after you do that, the next time this objection pops up n the conversation you know exactly how to answer it. In addition, off course you are not going to use the same wording, you brain will perfectly know how to adapt it if it is confidently set in the base of your memory.

If you do all of these right, I do not have to tell you that what will come next is pure magic! Your customer will simply decide to buy. You will be astonished by how easy you made them buy, that it took you only that particular sentence you have prepared all this time, to answer his objection. You made him give you his money in exchange for your solution. You fired your best shot, and you hit the jackpot!

Nevertheless Andrei Mungiu, what if he simply says: "Listen do not over talk me I know you are a good sales person but I simply need to think about it!"

Well you have it all written there, that is an objection, you will note it down and resolve as you have done for all the previous objections.

So get prepared to face objections, get prepared with a pen on paper! Do not leave your next conversation to chance; this is the mark of a true professional! Get mad! Do not be a spineless salesman who pretends he does not need money, you want money and the customer has it!

All you have to do is take it; do you have the balls to take it?

Focus on Income & Your Looks Not Your Costs

Save a penny here, and save a penny there and you can forget about becoming a millionaire.

If you save 5 dollars a day and have a bad breakfast instead of an awesome breakfast, you will gain one million in 547 years. So forget about saving your way to richness, forget about cutting out the good things in your life and decide to have a comfortable life instead.

What you should do is spend money that is worth on a daily comfortable lifestyle and cut costs on the major things, which prove useless and drain allot of money at one time.

Examples:

Instead of buying a brand new car, you can go along and get a second hand one. That should save you a big chunk of money right of the bet. Imagine how great you would look, how much more of a millionaire you would look and feel if you spent even 50% of those saved 10.000$ from the car, on your looks, then went to work the second day looking like a Hollywood star. I promise you, every single person in your office will start talking about you. You will score everyone's attention by default.

Cut costs on holidays. In fact, you should not even have any weekends if you are willing to get anywhere close to earning a million in the near future. Keep all money you save in a sacred, and I literally mean a kind of "don't touch or die trying" account. You must have an account that you will never touch, not even if somebody dies. Do not touch it until you will be ready to make a big investment that will secure your future and speed up your goal of making that first million.

Cutting costs on small things will make you feel scarce; it is a lucrative and time-consuming activity. You will never be able to walk; talk and look like a boss if all you do is bend over you pennies and count them every 5 seconds. If you want people to give you money you have to show them that you are worthy of it.

You have to show people that everything about you already speaks money. That people have given you their money before and continue doing it because you are trust worthy, because you are an expert at what you do and because ultimately they are going to receive more money and benefits back plus get to be in the company of a great and even magnificent person as you are!

If you do not want to invest money in your looks, you will not get any money from your customers or your boss. Everyone has money for a shirt and a new suit. It does not have to be a Tom Ford suit or anything like that, just get a normal new suit and let it work the magic on your body while bring you in money while you shine. You will get a Tom Ford suit eventually if you do all of the above..

Hear me now; stop worrying about small expenses and start feeling like a boss. You must start thinking how to save 10.000$ at one time, even 1.000$ at once or 100.000$ at once.

Stop worrying about what costs below 100$. I am telling you from my personal experience now; the first time I came to United Arab Emirates, I had the same mentality as so many others did. I used to save every penny. Then I remembered all the books I read on looks and how influential these can be. I went out and bought my first suitcase, the second day I came to work my manager approached me and asked whether I was looking forward to becoming a manager soon with a chuckle. He then told me how professional my new look was and how I reminded him about the importance of looks. I got his attention, and more than that now, he was looking up to me as an example of how to dress. Afterwards I went on and bought a suit fully tailored to my body parameters. After 2 months, I had an offer from a real estate company and my salary increased by 80%.

All I did was buy a suitcase and a new tailored suit. It cost me 500$, but it increased my income almost twice! Listen to this good old advice: Stop saving pennies, start saving millions!

Increase your revenue. As you have seen in this chapter, I have mentioned many times how all of my investments were contributing to the increase of my income, which was mostly commission on sales. You should do the same. Have it in your mind every day, write it on paper in the morning and write it on paper when you go to sleep so that you have it always in your mind. Whatever you do in this life do it to increase you earning ability.

You will earn a million faster by making 1000$ more per month than your current salary and spending all else on improving yourself, than by saving 1000$ a month from your current salary and keeping it in the bank.

Focus on earning rather than saving! If you have 1000$ in your hand, invest them by adding them to your sacred account for a final move! Strive to increase the inflow of money and forget about the outflow as long as it does not deplete your monthly salary in 1 day.

Here are some facts about millionaires, they spend, and millionaires are not frugal. They live in the best neighborhoods of the city and they connect with others that live there, they go to the best shows, have the best seats and again they connect with people that can afford them. The point here is not that you must spend MAX on everything, the point right here is that if you want to be the best you have to think and spend like the best!

You should stop saving and having the same salary for years, start investing and increase your income tomorrow!

There was once a hard working sales executive called Bob. Bob did everything he could to study the art of sales and all its' closing techniques. He worked day and night to figure how to close a sale. However, every time he came to work together with his colleagues he found that people were reluctant to approach him, especially his customers.

Bob did not like wearing a suit, it made him uncomfortable, he always wore his T-Shirt and Jeans. Moreover, if he did wear a suit, he would never close his last shirt button at the neck. Bob rarely ironed his shirt as well. More than that, wearing a tie was uncomfortable for him so he always found excuses not to wear it.

Consequently, because he looked so unprofessional, his clients more often asked for help from his pleasantly looking colleagues. No matter if he was the first to greet them at the door, sometimes the customer did not even reply him back. In some cases, in the middle of the conversation the customer would start speaking to another sales expert and ignore Bob who now felt so upset. Even after a customer would clearly see that Bob's colleagues knew less, the customers still continued to shop using their services and rejected Bob. Bob had no idea what was wrong, he read everything there was about closing the sale, he started feeling that his colleagues where stealing his customers, when in fact Bob was chasing them away with his looks.

This is what Bob did not know: Though closing the sales is very important, selling yourself to the customer is one of the first things he must have done to earn their trust. Than reach the moment, when closing the transaction is possible. Bob's only problem was the way he got dressed, and that problem was all he needed to fail.

If you find yourself in a situation with a similar problem as above, when the customer ignores you, it is most likely due to your first impression, your looks. Wouldn't you agree now that you will instantly skyrocket your sales when you learn to dress and look much better than Bob.

How can you do that?

Decide you are going to spend all that it takes to make you look AWESOME! Make sure you look as the top performer you are about to become. Since you do not get a chance to make a first impression twice and people judge you by the looks, visuals are the key to setting a solid foundation for a strong customer experience and ultimately a successful sale. Even before you open your mouth, the human brain automatically analyses your behavior and your visuals. This mechanism has evolved through millions of years.

Ever heard the age-old saying: "Dress for success". It says - dress the success. You become the image of success. Your outfit must scream the word "money" from the bottom of its lungs. Every small detail should give others a hint that you are a rich and affluent person. Your appearance should be the definition of a high performing expert whose' company pays him well for what he knows. Those who are speaking to you should consider themselves blessed to have the chance of meeting and knowing you. In other words, spend your money on your looks!

In order to succeed, you must be a professionally looking individual with a high sense of self-worth emanating from your clothing.

Spend your money on making your prospects happy, and they will bring you more. If you ever wish to have a chance of convincing customers against their will, you must dominate the atmosphere by the way you look, move & talk. Your boss is responsible for deciding to give or not give you a promotion. You have to look at least as good as him if you want the chance of being remembered as a worthy candidate. The only way you can be a rich person is by acting as a rich person. Rich men Spend!

Bob however, did not realize how his looks killed every chance of getting ahead, or at least having a chance to apply his knowledge into practice. His boss would have never looked at a person whose visuals have anything to do with the word "average". Like any other director, his boss needs the best; he wants people who can perform 24/7 consistently and at an excellent level. How could anyone ever hope that someone who cannot take care of himself will be able to handle much more demanding tasks?

Therefore, on what should have Bob spent his money. He could take the safe route first and look at what his managers have been wearing so far. People like, those who are similar to them.

Now do not get me wrong, in the event your employer comes to work like the one he goes on a Sunday pick nick this will never mean that you should do the same. Simply pick the TOP 10 most successful people in your company and dress like them for a start. Get to know the etiquette in your company, region and country of residence.

Standing out of the crowd is a good idea as long as you follow the basics and you do not break any formal or informal rules. For instance, if everyone at work wears a blue or white T-Shirt, it will generally be a bad idea to come dressed up in a one of red color. You do not want to be the clown in the show. Well you get the picture, right? Strive to be different within the rules.

Going further, you can play with the accessories as much as you want. Add some extra small twists like a handkerchief or a reputable watch. A fake one will also do, just make sure it is expensive enough to be a good replica, not from plastic. Most importantly remember to shave regularly or keep your beard trimmed; it is details, which make all the difference.

Invest in your health, your skin, your teeth and everything that a customer can see on you is part of your image. As a rule of thumb, your best bet would be to start improving the things that occupy the visual space on your body like your suit, your shirt, your shoes, and the tie. Work on the small and powerful details that your accessories represent.

Now you are ready to dress for success, let this chapter be your first major change. After all, it does not take much skills and it will be the most noticed element about you back at work. Do not be afraid to invest a little bit of money, the return on investment from your looks is priceless.

Your look are only a small part of the story, if you will develop an eye for weeding out things that cost nothing but give you everything you will be amazed at how much you where loosing so far just to save 10$ a day. Costs are your last concern, since costs are the main driving force for creating or providing anything.

Think about it, can you picture yourself generating at least 100$ without spending anything? I mean literally on anything. You will probably die within the first month if you decide not to spend at all. You must understand that it takes money to make money; it takes you to invest in something to get something out of it.

The main problem that you must solve is in what to invest and how much. You need to have a strategy of managing your costs in such a way that they bring you in more money. I am not going to say that you should absolutely cut costs on anything that does not generate a profit, by all means do enjoy yourself especially if you have a family, because happiness will bring you money as well.

What I am saying is that you have to develop the habit of planning everything, of committing to excellence in building your budget. Do the math; it is amazing how many people these days just lack the knowledge of how to calculate their budget. In addition, they do not lack mathematical knowledge, they simply lack desire to get it done.

Unless you are going to have it in front of your face like all other things we mentioned before, you are not going to achieve anything. When you write something down, it is as if it became a hundred times more powerful. Not because it give you some skill, but because it makes you aware of what is happening.

I started building my budget the first time I left my home and went to university. I knew from experience, that my life is my business and that I am self-employed. Just like an organization, I have costs that are variable, meaning that these come and go. In addition, costs that are fixed, meaning those are most likely to be the same for the next month and the others to come.

My costs example when I started in Dubai:

I knew that from my salary of 6000 AED that I had at that time I used to pay 2000 a month for the rent, I was spending not more than 100 AED on transportation per month, not more than 1500 AED on food and I used to leave myself another 500 AED for household and medicine. So by the end I knew that if I stick to what I have written which meant I could spend an X amount on food per day, by the end of the month I would have almost 30% of my salary still in my pocket. Now let us be honest, how many times have you had 30% of your salary left at the end of the month? Not that often.

You need to calculate your expenses. Let me tell you how simply calculating your expenses will help you spend in the correct direction versus spend less on things you do not need and end up with no money and things you do not need at the end of the month.

As soon as you start keeping track of you budget, magic will start happening. You will automatically start thinking about every investment you make that day. When you will go to the supermarket you will no longer buy chips and coke for 100$ and then end up being hungry again in the evening or even worse with a stomachache. You will know that money is for food and there is a separate budget for having fun.

Not only will you start living healthier but also you will start gaining benefits from your money. Instead of throwing those 100$ on chips and coke you will end up putting them together with the remaining ones in your "sacred account" which we have talked about in this book. You will no longer look to buy a new smartphone if you already have one with all the necessary functions. You will start understanding how 1000$ can get you real money by investing them or keeping them away for future investment instead of simply upgrading to stay up with the trend.

You must have a smart phone and connect with the entire world. Fact, you have to beat down social media into oblivion. Nevertheless, buying a new phone while the old one still gives you the same functions makes no sense. Moreover, we all know that people are big, I mean big spenders on gadgets. We buy every useless cool thing that there is on planet earth if we cannot control our desire. I remember how I ended up once buying these useless bracelets that count how many footsteps you make during the day, how you sleep, and what your heart rate is. I threw at it 200$, just to have my lovely wife Valeria save me from this dumb purchase by reminding me the second day how unreasonable that purchase was, I went out and bought a regular heart rate reader instead which was 4 times cheaper, that is all I needed.

If you want to stay fit, just go and run for one hour. Do not ask someone how many footsteps you made during the day, if you go to your limits buy a simple regular heart rate reader that is more than enough even for professional athletes.

Do not ask someone to tell you how you have slept if you know you are dead tired every morning you wake up; you do not need a device to tell you "hey, you know what, I think you are tired." Do you really need to spend 200$ and accept that a device is smarter than you are in terms of knowing what you want? If you do, let me tell you this:

If you do not know what you want yourself or what you have to do to improve your own wellbeing, you can forget about achieving excellence and big heights anyways. This is just the start. Do you know what it takes to manage four companies at the same time while taking care of your family?

There are no shortcuts for staying fit, no device can improve life, and there is nothing more powerful than the power of your will. Spend your money on something that will make an impact on your future, do not deposit every penny and be frugal. Spend much, and spend on useful things!

Focus on income, not costs, direct you money to places that bring you money and you will never have to think about how much you spend even once for the rest of your life!

Sleep Well

If there is one thing that will get your performance up overnight, it is sleep. There is nothing in this book or in this world, which can alter your performance faster, especially as a salesman.

Your career is revolving around communication. This means your enthusiasm, your emotions, your gestures, your tone of voice and your energy will directly influence the outcome of any sales conversation. When I first started working in the UAE, for the first time in my life my schedule was so crazy that one day I had to close the store at 1.00 at night and open it the second day at 8.30 in the morning.

You might have it even worse, but the point here is different. During the days when I had poor sleep, which continued for about half a year, my sales where average. Much worse, sometimes I would not sell anything for the entire day. I would blame the footfall, that there are no customers and that the products are bad. I would go into the back of the store and drink a cup of water; I would come back and still feel tired. Lack of sleep started slowly but steadily killing my career. Even though I already knew professional techniques for opening conversations and closing sales, all of these were powerless in front of my willingness to sleep.

Until one day, I have received a complaint. Oh at that moment I knew it was BAD, I knew someone up there from my managers was not happy with my performance even though I thought about myself as being the best. That day, I decided: Come high water and big winds I will get at least 8 hours of sleep before I go to work. In addition, if it is impossible to do, I will go to sleep after work and compensate for those with immediate extra hours of sleep.

I had one small little trick on letting my brain and body rest for as much as it needed. I knew I was usually sleeping about 8 to 8.5 hours. Therefore, every day I went to sleep leaving myself 9 hours before the alarm would sound. That way I generally slept as much as I needed and woke up naturally.

Oh the feeling of waking up without an alarm. It instantly reminded me about my careless childhood when I had nothing to do during the summer vacation time. I felt a happy man every time I woke up. I felt that I was the best in this world and I had all the energy to prove it. I went to work and my sudden energy made everyone question what happened. My colleagues started asking me if I fell in love and is said "YES", I fell in love with sleep.

I greeted customers with big smiles and was so happy that they entered the store. When they were not, there I was happy to have the time to prepare myself and the store for the next visit, or do something extra in the stock room and boost my reputation. I was happy about whatever I had to do.

That level of high energy allowed me to accomplish much more work during the day, my past mistakes with handling cash vanished immediately. I was a new man, someone everyone liked. Because my attitude was so positive the customers where much more open to me, I built trust with them much easier so I closed sales much faster. Everyone was happy.

Going to sleep at least 9 hours before I have to wake up changed my life.

It was so easy. There was no need to improve any skills, no need to learn anything new or further educate myself on body language. Sleep made everything fall back into its place. Even my learning capabilities became so much greater. The aura of energy was all around me. I could not believe that for so many months I had dreadful results just because of this, just because of my improper sleep and time management.

Hear me now fellow salesman, get a sufficient amount of sleep! You need to sleep so much that you wake up without an alarm.

It is easy to follow, gives the greatest rewards instantly, GET PROPER SLEEP.

Do not take all of the motivational talks that say you must not sleep 3 days. Do not either think that you can get away with sleeping only 5 hours every day? That is an absolute nonsense. Sleep is something that our body has always been doing throughout the years of evolution. Our brain needs to rest in order to perform. And just like a muscle, if your brain will not rest its performance will be poor.

Get some sleep, and watch your life and sales skyrocket overnight!

Example:

Just before yesterday, I had a tough day at work with many things to do, I managed to complete all the important A tasks but off course I wished I could get more done. Therefore, as I come home, tired and preparing to go to sleep suddenly I received a notification about an ongoing online sales seminar. In my mind, it did not matter that I finished work at midnight that day and I had to go back in the morning at 08.00 AM. Even if it was 2.00 AM, the sales seminars are a source of knowledge. Therefore, off course, I attended it. I ended up going to sleep at 4.00 A.M., slept to hours and went to work like a zombie the second day. After work, I came home and tried pushing myself to complete one of my "A" grade tasks for that day, "write several chapters" which I have planned for my book. As I struggled to write half a page in 2 hours, I finally understood that I had to sleep if I was ever going to get it done. I just could not afford to lose so much time for half a page. By now, you probably realize that even though the seminar was important, the tasks on which I missed out the second day where even more so. Again, lack of sleep was the problem.

I went to bed as early as 8.00 PM the second night, slept 10 hours and woke up two hours before leaving for work. In those two hours, I have managed to restructure the chapters of the book and input new fresh ideas, which I will later continue to develop.

Not only did I do that, I have written two times more than I usually do in that timeframe. At the end, with a big smile and sense of accomplishment I went to work. Came back, set down and did the same thing again with such an enthusiasm that I could not believe.

Giving up on sleep to manage more work never works. If you want to achieve great things. Which means doing them excellently, you have to have good sleep? Your brain I better off sleeping two hours more in the morning and going to bed two hours earlier at night, than win some two hours of work at night doing absolutely nothing with them but searching for coffee and being distracted by the fact that you're tired.

So sleep well. Do not listen to what others say about 5 hours sleep being enough. They do that to express how busy they are and how important time is. What they actually do, is sleep as much as they need and then make sure to use efficiently the time while being awake.

THAT, is their ultimate formula to success, which is how they achieve greatness. But they won't say that on TV because it is too complicated for the average person to understand, an too simple for the television to want to publish it. **Sleep well and watch yourself be a PRO the second day!**

Your Goals & Company Resources

Can you feel how the subject? Can you feel how the book thinks about YOUR benefits? Now let us get to it!

Before we start discussing how we can legally use the company resources to develop ourselves as sales experts, we have to know what the resources a company offers us are. Isn't that true?

Throughout my career, I have discovered many types of these resources and many ways in which you could use them. As experiences came to me in bigger quantities, I gradually understood this concept better and refined it down to the following.

Resources a company provides you are:

1. **The Customer**

2. **The Product**

3. **The Company Politics**

4. **The Colleagues**

These 4 resources are your daily bread and butter. Without them, your job does not exist. You cannot go anywhere without these resources. Let us see what each offers!

1 – The Customer. Customers are the #1 resource provided to you by your company. Now you might think... hey I wanted something material, I wanted to USE IT! Well let me tell you, there is nothing more material than a person with money walking into you. Moreover, there is nothing you can use more than his or her money. You get the picture.

Why is the customer the #1 resource provided to you by the company?

First of all a customer is your source of income. The company does not give you a job, your customer does. Your job is to solve their problems. The company does not give you money, your customer does, than the company shares a piece of it with you. More than that, the company will definitely never give you real life practice; the poor customer is your test subject. Again, and again, and again. Can you see to what extent, if you view it the right way, you can use a simple person walking into your store?

The customer is your main resource, learn to use it well, and learn to use it effectively without wasting it in vain. Effectively means getting the result, getting the deal closed. Because we all know, at the end of the day, it all comes down to whether they give you the money for your solution to their problem or not. Not mentioning they gave you so much of their time already and you had so many possibilities to practice everything you have learned from books on them. Customers are your #1 resource!

2 – The Product. The second greatest resource, you will ever have in any company. The product is always there at your disposal, compared to the customers that come and go. Your company provides you with the full range of products and services that they are offering. A legitimate question now would be:

"How are the products and services of my company a resource, and how can I use them? Isn't it something the customer will use? "

Correct! The products are first destined for the customer. However, while these are on the shelves, you can benefit by gathering valuable knowledge about them. Think about it this way: You are selling for example a luxury watch with a minimum price of 5000$, plus ready to wear products and apparel in the same price range. You do not have to pay a dime to use them, at least temporarily. You can inspect them all day long. The company paid astronomic amounts of money to have them available in stock. You do not need to pay 5000$ for one watch to look at it only one day. You have all the time you want studying the watch, the materials it is made from. You can study how it fits and what would be a good complimentary product for it by practicing. Not only do you have access to a stock worth huge amounts of money, you have real life access to materials that may never be taught in a book. You have access to materials that will give you an immeasurable amount of knowledge and a winning edge in closing the sale with your customer. In addition, knowledge, builds confidence!

Not only can you learn about the product. You can do what others never had a chance to. You can look back at what objections your customers usually give you during the sale, and by looking at the product while remembering those, you can come up with 100% effective, real time answers to their objections having the product in your hands. Your product is your second greatest resource in terms of knowledge and practice. Use it wisely, extract all the knowledge you can from it and apply it in your daily conversations. Only when you can truly value the products you have in your store will you truly be sold on them and understand how to convince your prospects to buy it! There is no easy way around it; you have to learn about your product. In addition, there is no reason for you not to, it stands near you at least 8 hours a day 5 days a week.

3 Company politics – The most unseen and undiscussed resource of all. This is the cause of broken and fulfilled dreams. Company politics is thought to be the underdog of any career. Many of us dislike and even hate it, others pretend to ignore it. Only a few of us, know how to swim the troubled waters of this subject.

Look back at any Sales Expert or Vice President or C.E.O. of any company. I am sure as a sales executive you at least once thought about how "false and theatrical" they are. How their behavior does not mirror what they really feel inside, and even though everyone thought pulling of such acting skills would be impossible they somehow do it, and the do it very subtly.

Well if you want to get anywhere close to being a sales expert and moving UP with your career, you had better learn how to act. Say it is wrong, say it is fake, and say it is unethical. Countless articles on the internet show that to convince yourself about anything you do not feel now, the first step is to act as if it is already happening, everything else will follow. Our connection between body and mind is very strong, if your body will insist that it feels good your mind will follow. Be careful though, it applies backwards the same.

This acting skill is exactly what successful sales experts have mastered, before they became experts and advanced their career.

Company politics is very similar to politics at larger scales. I revolves around unspoken and unseen rules, around inevitable gossips and how you handle these.

To learn how to benefit from such a subtle yet powerful resource, you must understand one thing first. You are selling yourself, your skills and your experiences, to everyone around you, every single day. Selling yourself is about knowing what people around you are looking for, and then presenting them your features and benefits in a way that matches their needs. This is allot tougher than it sounds so I will write it again. Sell yourself with greater enthusiasm, effort and skills than anything else you have sold in your life. Consequently, everyone around you will start offering the commission of speaking well about your skills and idealizing your practices as the example others must follow. All you have to do is show that what you give, is worth MORE than what they provide in return.

What does all this mean in practice? Here are a few examples:

At work, greet everyone with a big smile saying their name, stop and ask there and then how their day is going, and wait for an answer. – If you have not done this for a long time, do it anyway. In the beginning, it might be awkward. However, as people get used to it their impression about you will change dramatically.

When you are assigned to do a task, make sure you act exactly as your responsibilities allow you to. Do not pretend to be the boss unless you were asked to, do not ask for anybody's help unless it is impossible for you to complete the assigned job yourself.

Help everyone around you without asking if they need help. We are all constantly assigned to do certain tasks and from time to time, we all are afraid to ask for help. Thinking it would ruin our reputation as an expert. Do you remember how good it feels, when someone comes and helps you without a word? Without asking if you need help or asking for your appreciation afterwards? That was a memorable moment wasn't it.

There are many more examples. What you should understand by now is that company politics is about being warm as the sun at appearance and have your moves calculated sharply as pilot behind the curtains. Company politics is like playing your character in a movie, you have to master the role and hide the efforts when the director yells "CUT", company politic is ultimately about how you sell yourself.

4 Your colleagues – Quiet honestly, when you practice your skills with your customers, or learn from your products, or create an image about yourself in the company, you are doing a great job. However, what if you could double that instantly, what if you could take the knowledge you accumulate during 7 days in 1 day. On the other hand, 7 months in one month. Even 70% of that in such a short time would be great, wouldn't you agree? Well, I have the secret to such success exposed up next:

"Good men learn from their mistake, wise men learn from others as well."

The same way you must learn how to "LEARN" from your colleagues observations. No wonder we keep hearing: "Tell me who your friends are and I will tell you who you are".

Spend time with the best salesman in your company, get along with the best salesman in your country or even the whole industry on the globe, the only limit is your imagination. The more you communicate with these kind of people the better.

For example: Yesterday, at work, one of my colleagues pointed out to me that since I am writing this book I became too focused on building the whole customer relationship thing, and sometimes forgot that some of them just want to buy and you should close them instantly.

The point here is, even as an expert you still need feedback from outside observers. You need to actively exchange ideas and findings with professional salesman.

You must speak with as many skilled people from your industry as possible. This will enable you to have their inputs, to receive the information they have gathered after so many years of experience in your field.

Think about it for a second. You can have access to all the information in such a short period and they are so willing to share it. All you have to do is figure a way to make them talk and then listen. Listen as if it is the last thing you will hear in your life. Because to be honest, it is probably the last time, you hear that opinion.

Everyone is unique and everyone has their own view, chances are every conversation you will have with someone about your job or product or anything connected to the previous will give you unique and sometimes even never heard of before insights.

Your colleagues can tell you about not only products, customer service, sales techniques and your upper management. **Your colleagues will inevitably share with you information regarding what others think about you, what your position in the company politics currently is and how they think you should adjust it.**

Under no circumstances am I saying that all those advices are going to be valid and correct. Far from it, should you follow them? On the contrary, you should take every bit of information and keep it in your head as an archive. Gather a little bit of feedback from here and there and then put them all together like a puzzle. The result will be quiet simple. Whatever you hear most often in your circles is usually the truth or the perceived public truth. What you will do about it is up to you, but do put it to good use considering everything you will learn in this book.

5 Your colleagues are your spies and they do not even know about it. Your job is to create such a vast and strong net that nothing escapes your knowledge and that you are aware of everything that is happening.

Stop Yelling & Start Selling

www.ingramcontent.com/pod-product-compliance
Lightning Source LLC
Chambersburg PA
CBHW020922180526
45163CB00007B/2849